Application Development with Swift

Develop highly efficient and appealing iOS applications
by using the Swift language

Hossam Ghareeb

BIRMINGHAM - MUMBAI

Application Development with Swift

First published: August 2015

Production reference: 1250815

Published by Packt Publishing Ltd.
Livery Place
35 Livery Street
Birmingham B3 2PB, UK.

ISBN 978-1-78528-817-3

www.packtpub.com

Credits

Author
Hossam Ghareeb

Reviewers
Tyler Hackbart
David Mattia
Hossam M. Sherif
Kenneth Strickland

Commissioning Editor
Julian Ursell

Acquisition Editor
Nikhil Karkal

Content Development Editor
Shali Deeraj

Technical Editor
Prajakta Mhatre

Copy Editor
Charlotte Carneiro

Project Coordinator
Kinjal Bari

Proofreader
Safis Editing

Indexer
Tejal Soni

Graphics
Sheetal Aute
Disha Haria

Production Coordinator
Melwyn D'sa

Cover Work
Melwyn D'sa

About the Author

Hossam Ghareeb is a software engineer who graduated from the computer and system engineering department of Alexandria University in 2012. Currently, he is an iOS software engineer at Prototype Interactive in Dubai. He has a lot of experience in iOS development and software engineering; he always keeps himself up to date with new technologies. It is his passion to help people by sharing his experience and writing tutorials to get people engaged quickly without problems. His favorite hobbies are fishing and playing video games, especially FIFA and PES. If you need his help or wish to go fishing with him, then you can contact him at hossam.ghareb@gmail.com.

I would like to thank each and every person who has been helpful to me, from my teaching staff to my friends. A special thanks to my lovely wife, Amira, for all her support and encouragement in spite of all the time this book kept me away from her. I thank my son, Yusuf, for inspiring me. I would also like to express my sincere gratitude toward my parents for teaching me how to be a good person.

Last but not least, I would like to thank the content editors, Shali Deeraj and Nikhil Karkal, for helping me and being nice to me, and the reviewers for their helpful comments and suggestions.

About the Reviewers

Tyler Hackbart is a web developer, designer, and technology enthusiast with a passion for everything in technology. Through self-learning, he gained the ability to write his first line of code when he was only 16 years old and has just started learning his sixth programming language. With his farm-raised work ethic, alongside a passion for crafting amazing user interactions and doing what he loves, Tyler has successfully worked in the technology field for 2 years. He is the cofounder of three start-ups and works in an application design firm, all based in Waterloo, Canada.

David Mattia is a student at the University of Notre Dame with a passion for software engineering. He has worked for General Electric Aviation and spends much of his free time doing freelance work.

Hossam M. Sherif is a software developer. He received his bachelor's degree in computer and system engineering from Alexandria University. He has spent several years in software development, especially in iOS and backend development. He has worked with many companies, such as Insidetrack, Inova LLC, and Log n Labs. He worked on different projects and in different roles, from software developer to team leader and manager. He served in the Egyptian Navy and participated in the enhancement and development of the IT department. He has certificates in software test processes and software test design. He participated in several volunteer projects and workshops as an instructor for "Introduction to iOS Development," a summer 2014 training course for undergraduates at Alexandria University, and also other courses, such as the Alexandria Startup 2012 weekend and IEEE ITW 2011.

Kenneth Strickland joined the US Army in 1986. After 4 years of active duty in the US Army, he came across software development. That was when he picked up his first C programming book and read it from cover to cover. Since then, he has never looked back.

He has been a software architect for over 10 years, and currently develops applications primarily in C/C++, Java, Objective-C, Swift, and .NET.

You can visit his website at `http://kenster.guru`.

www.PacktPub.com

Support files, eBooks, discount offers, and more

For support files and downloads related to your book, please visit www.PacktPub.com.

Did you know that Packt offers eBook versions of every book published, with PDF and ePub files available? You can upgrade to the eBook version at www.PacktPub.com and as a print book customer, you are entitled to a discount on the eBook copy. Get in touch with us at service@packtpub.com for more details.

At www.PacktPub.com, you can also read a collection of free technical articles, sign up for a range of free newsletters and receive exclusive discounts and offers on Packt books and eBooks.

https://www2.packtpub.com/books/subscription/packtlib

Do you need instant solutions to your IT questions? PacktLib is Packt's online digital book library. Here, you can search, access, and read Packt's entire library of books.

Why subscribe?

- Fully searchable across every book published by Packt
- Copy and paste, print, and bookmark content
- On demand and accessible via a web browser

Free access for Packt account holders

If you have an account with Packt at www.PacktPub.com, you can use this to access PacktLib today and view 9 entirely free books. Simply use your login credentials for immediate access.

Table of Contents

Preface

This book teaches you how to master the Swift programming language and use it in building apps with the new technologies introduced in iOS 8. Swift is a new programming language for iOS, OS X, and watchOS apps. In the beginning of this book, we will give you an advanced introduction to Swift, and then we will see how to apply this in real-app demos using the new technologies and APIs in iOS 8 such as TouchID, watchOS, Metal, and HealthKit.

What this book covers

Chapter 1, *Hello Swift*, gives a quick introduction and revision about Swift. This chapter is very important for Swift beginners and is highly recommended for Swift developers to revise their knowledge.

Chapter 2, *Advanced Swift*, boosts your Swift experience by allowing you to learn some advanced features in Swift. In this chapter, we will talk about protocols, extensions, and memory management.

Chapter 3, *Touch ID*, gives your app a new flavor of authentication using Touch ID. Users can now use their fingerprint to sign in to your app without needing to write their username and password.

Chapter 4, *Introduction to HealthKit*, teaches you how to work with HealthKit and how to share or read health data in the native Health app. If you have any apps or ideas about health or fitness, you should give this chapter a shot.

Chapter 5, *Introduction to Metal*, introduces a cutting edge technology for 3D GPU-accelerated graphics in iOS.

Chapter 6, *Introduction to WatchKit*, introduces a new device for you – the Apple watch. You will learn all the new technologies needed to build apps for the Apple watch and get your app prepared to exist on users wrists.

Chapter 7, Swift App Extensions, teaches you how to let your users use the app even if your app is not open, using app extensions. App extensions let you extend your app's functionality outside your app and users can access it using system or third-party apps.

What you need for this book

To work on this book, some programming experience is expected. Having experience with Objective-C and iOS development will help you a lot while working with this book. You will also need a Mac OS with Xcode 6+ installed.

Who this book is for

If you are an iOS developer with experience in Objective-C, and wish to develop applications with Swift, then this book is ideal for you. Familiarity with the fundamentals of Swift is an added advantage but not a necessity.

Conventions

In this book, you will find a number of text styles that distinguish between different kinds of information. Here are some examples of these styles and an explanation of their meaning.

Code words in text, database table names, folder names, filenames, file extensions, pathnames, dummy URLs, user input, and Twitter handles are shown as follows: "In Swift, you use `var` for variables, and `let` for constants."

A block of code is set as follows:

```
var count = 5
var msg : String
var total : Double = 0
```

When we wish to draw your attention to a particular part of a code block, the relevant lines or items are set in bold:

```
Protocol <protocol1, protocol2,…>
```

New terms and **important words** are shown in bold. Words that you see on the screen, for example, in menus or dialog boxes, appear in the text like this: "Xcode helps you with this by providing the **history** button in the results sidebar, on the line of the number of times."

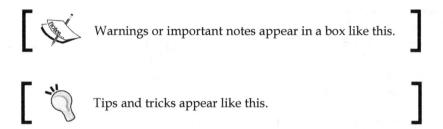

[Warnings or important notes appear in a box like this.]

[Tips and tricks appear like this.]

Reader feedback

Feedback from our readers is always welcome. Let us know what you think about this book—what you liked or disliked. Reader feedback is important for us as it helps us develop titles that you will really get the most out of.

To send us general feedback, simply e-mail feedback@packtpub.com, and mention the book's title in the subject of your message.

If there is a topic that you have expertise in and you are interested in either writing or contributing to a book, see our author guide at www.packtpub.com/authors.

Customer support

Now that you are the proud owner of a Packt book, we have a number of things to help you to get the most from your purchase.

Downloading the example code

You can download the example code files from your account at http://www.packtpub.com for all the Packt Publishing books you have purchased. If you purchased this book elsewhere, you can visit http://www.packtpub.com/support and register to have the files e-mailed directly to you.

Errata

Although we have taken every care to ensure the accuracy of our content, mistakes do happen. If you find a mistake in one of our books—maybe a mistake in the text or the code—we would be grateful if you could report this to us. By doing so, you can save other readers from frustration and help us improve subsequent versions of this book. If you find any errata, please report them by visiting http://www.packtpub.com/submit-errata, selecting your book, clicking on the **Errata Submission Form** link, and entering the details of your errata. Once your errata are verified, your submission will be accepted and the errata will be uploaded to our website or added to any list of existing errata under the Errata section of that title.

To view the previously submitted errata, go to https://www.packtpub.com/books/content/support and enter the name of the book in the search field. The required information will appear under the **Errata** section.

Piracy

Piracy of copyrighted material on the Internet is an ongoing problem across all media. At Packt, we take the protection of our copyright and licenses very seriously. If you come across any illegal copies of our works in any form on the Internet, please provide us with the location address or website name immediately so that we can pursue a remedy.

Please contact us at copyright@packtpub.com with a link to the suspected pirated material.

We appreciate your help in protecting our authors and our ability to bring you valuable content.

Questions

If you have a problem with any aspect of this book, you can contact us at questions@packtpub.com, and we will do our best to address the problem.

1
Hello Swift

Welcome to the developing applications with Swift book. It's my pleasure to talk about iOS development and Swift. This book assumes that you have some basic experience in iOS development, and a little experience of using Swift. If you don't have any experience of Swift, don't worry, just go ahead with us and be prepared to master the iOS development using Swift. I believe in learning by example methodology and, starting from *Chapter 3, Touch ID*, we will introduce the new technology of iOS 8, and write a simple demo on it using Swift.

In this chapter, we will talk about the Swift programming language, and get our hands dirty with Swift. If you are familiar with Swift, you can either skip this chapter, or you can review your Swift knowledge. We will talk about the Swift language and its features, and how to try it using Playgrounds in Xcode 6. Playground is a new, awesome, and innovative feature that allows you to try any piece of code, and see the results without explicitly running, or even compiling your code. You will become familiar with the code structure, and some important data types such as arrays, dictionaries, and so on.

Introduction to Swift

Swift is a new (Apple has open sourced it!), scripting, programming language for developing apps for iOS, OS X, and watchOS. Apple has introduced this language to make things easier and fun. Unlike Objective-C, Swift is not a superset of C programming language. But believe me, it has the power of both C and Objective-C.

It's the first time we have an alternative to Objective-C, since Apple introduced iOS and OSX development tools. As a new programming language, Swift introduces many new features and concepts that did not exist in Objective-C, and we will talk about them in next sections. For Objective-C developers, Swift will be familiar to them, as it adopts the readability of Objective-C's named parameters. Swift is a friendly programming language. It is so expressive and funny even for new programmers who have no experience with Objective-C.

Like Objective-C, Swift is an OOP language and you can easily create classes, objects, methods, and properties. Swift is built to make developers write safe code, and you will feel this when you will start working with it. An example of this is that you can't use variables without initialization. Swift saves you from making silly errors that you could make, such as using variables before initialization.

Don't hesitate to work with Swift, and give it a shot. Swift co-exists alongside your existing Objective-C code, and is easy to work with. You can also replace your existing Objective-C code with Swift, or start your project from scratch with Swift as your primary development language.

Make sure that you are familiar with Swift features to feel its power, and enjoy it. Some of these features are new for Objective-C developers, and these will let you love Swift, as I do:

- Closures
- Tuples
- Range operators
- Generics
- Structures
- Functional programming patterns

Playgrounds

We mentioned the Playground feature earlier — it is a new innovative feature supported in Xcode 6 and higher. It gives you the ability to try any piece of code in Swift, and see the results immediately without the need to compile or run the code. So, imagine that you are learning Swift, or working in a project with Swift, and you need to try some code, and check its result. If you are in Objective-C, you need to create a new project, write the code, build, run, and open the simulator to see the results! Very time consuming, isn't it? I mean, it's time consuming here, in the learning track, but after you master the language, you don't need to use Playgrounds. You may just need to use it in test or to check something. To play with the Playground feature use the following steps:

1. In Swift and Xcode 6, or higher, just create a new playground (as shown in the following screenshot) or open an existing one by choosing the `.playground` file in a navigator:

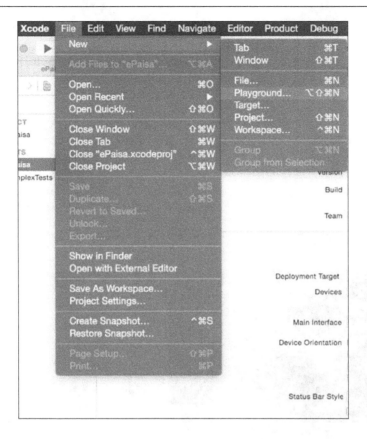

2. Now, enter Swift code in the `.playground` file, and enjoy the results in the right-hand side sidebar. Xcode evaluates your code while you type it, and for each statement, Xcode displays the results of it in the right-hand side sidebar.

```
1  // Playground - noun: a place where
      people can play
2
3  import UIKit
4
5  var str = "Hello, playground"          "Hello, playground"
6  var i = 5                              5
7  for j in 0...7
8  {
9      i += j                             (8 times)
10 }
11 i                                      33
12
```

As you see, each line of code is examined, and its result is shown in the results sidebar, in the right-hand side. Even the `for` loop statement shows you how many times the entire code was executed. To see the value of any variable, just write it in a separate line, and check its value in the right-hand side sidebar. (Check line 11 in the preceding screenshot).

Another feature of Playground is the **value history**. In the previous `for` loop, we have a piece of code that is executed repeatedly, right? But I want to know what is going on in each iteration. Xcode helps you with this by providing the **history** button in the results sidebar, on the line containing the number of times. Once you click on it, it displays a complete graph (timeline) for the values over the time. In the graph, *x* axis represents time, and *y* axis represents the value at this time (this iteration).

Once you click on the circle in the results view, you can see the value of this iteration:

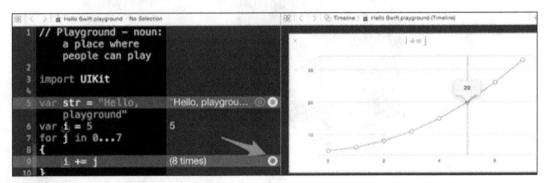

Also, keep in mind that Playground includes the standard editing features of Xcode, such as code completion, error checking, syntax correction, and suggestions.

The code structure

Before starting to write Swift, you have to be aware of its structure, as it is a very important thing to know in any programming language.

As we said earlier, Swift is not a superset of C. For sure it's influenced by C and Objective-C but easier and fun to use than both.

I will share with you a piece of code in Swift to show its structure:

```
import UIKit

let pi = 3.14
//Display all even numbers from 0 to 10
```

```
for i in 0...10
{
    if i % 2 == 0
    {
        println("\(i) is even")
    }
}

func sayHello(name: String = "there")
{

    println("Hello \(name)")
}

sayHello(name: "John") // will print "Hello John"
sayHello() //Will print "Hello there", based on default value
```

> **Downloading the example code**
>
> You can download the example code files from your account at
> http://www.packtpub.com for all the Packt Publishing books you
> have purchased. If you purchased this book elsewhere, you can visit
> http://www.packtpub.com/support and register to have the files
> e-mailed direct to you.

If you check this code, you will find that we don't use semicolons. This is because in Swift they are optional. However, compiler will not complain if you do use them. The only area where semicolons are required is when you write multiple statements in the same line.

In Swift, you use `var` for variables, and `let` for constants; but this doesn't mean that Swift is not a typed language. The compiler, based on the initial value, identifies the type implicitly. But in some cases, you have to write the type if you don't set an initial value; or the initial value is not sufficient to identify the type.

Consider the following code for example:

```
var count = 5
var msg : String
var total : Double = 0
```

In this code, the `count` variable is of the `Int` type, because its initial value is in integer. In the `msg` variable, we didn't set an initial value, so we will have to explicitly write the type of the `msg` variable. The same is applicable for `total`; we need it to be of the `Double` type but as its initial value is not sufficient, the compiler will consider it as `Int`.

In Swift, you will see that there is no main function to start with, as the code written in the global scope is considered as the start of your program. So, you can imagine that a single line of code in Swift can be considered as a program!

The last thing I want to mention is that curly braces are very important in Swift, as they are mandatory in any control flow statements, such as if, while, and so on.

Arrays

An array is every developer's best friend and saves the collection of data in an ordered list. In Swift, an array is very easy to use and contains many helpful methods for use. Before exploring it, we have to clarify some important points.

Array by default is mutable so that it accepts adding, changing, or removing items from it, except if we define it as a constant, using `let`. In this case, it will be immutable, as it becomes constant.

In Objective-C, you can save any type of object, and you won't have to specify any information about their type. In Swift, arrays are typed; this means that the type of item should be clear, and all the items should be of the same type. The type can be defined explicitly, or it can be inferred.

An array doesn't have to be of a class type. So, you can create an array of `Int`, and in such a case, you can't insert any other value than the `Int` type.

The following are examples to make these points clear:

```
let languages = ["Arabic", "English", "French"]
//Here type is inferred as String, So this Array is of type String
//Also this array is immutable as it defined as let

var primes :[Int] = [2, 3, 5, 7, 11]
//Type is written explicitly

primes.append(13) //mutable array as it defined as var
```

Initializing an array

To initialize and create an array, you can use the previous ways with initial values, or you can either create it empty, or by using repeating values:

```
//=========================== Initializing =========
var array = [Int]() //new empty array of type Int          0 elements
array.append(10) //add 10                                  [10]
array = [] //clear array                                   0 elements

var threeOnes = [Int](count: 3, repeatedValue: 1)          [1, 1, 1]
//Array with 3 values with same value 1
var twoFives = [Int](count: 2, repeatedValue: 5)           [5, 5]
var total = threeOnes + twoFives // sum of two arrays gives new array   [1, 1, 1, 5, 5]

//===================
```

As you see in the example, it's very easy to initialize empty arrays, or arrays with repeating values. Swift also provides a great feature to append two arrays that result in a new array.

Iterating over arrays

The explanation is not complete without mentioning how to iterate over an array. Actually, iterating over an array in Swift is very easy and straightforward. To iterate over values of an array, you will use the for-in loop like this:

```
var seasons = ["Winter", "Spring", "Summer", "Autumn"]

for season in seasons{
    println(season)
}
/*
Winter
Spring
Summer
Autumn
*/
```

And if you want the index of the value in each iteration, you can use the enumerate method. In each iteration, the method returns a tuple that is composed of an index and value of each item in the array. Check the next example to make things clear:

```
for (index, season) in enumerate(seasons){

    println("Season #\(index + 1) is \(season)")
}
```

```
/*
Season #1 is Winter
Season #2 is Spring
Season #3 is Summer
Season #4 is Autumn
*/
```

For all those who don't know tuples, tuples in Swift are used to create and pass around a group of values. It can be used to return multiple values from a function in a single group.

Appending items

You can append items easily by using the `append` method, which appends an item at the end of an array. To append multiple items at once, append an array of these items.

You can also use the `insert` method that inserts items at a specific location.

```
var nums = [1, 3]             // [1, 3]
nums.append(4)               // [1, 3, 4]
nums.insert(5, atIndex: 1) // [1, 5, 3, 4]
nums += [10, 11]             // [1, 5, 3, 4, 10, 11]
```

Removing and updating items

An array has a built-in `removeAtIndex` function to remove an item at the index and a `removeLast` function to remove the last item. These functions are awesome. While you call them, they return the deleted item at the same time and thus, you don't have to write another line of code to grab the item before deleting it.

```
nums.removeAtIndex(1) // return 5
nums.removeLast()     // return 11
nums                  // [1, 3, 4, 10]
nums[0...2] = []      // array now is [10]
```

In this code we removed an item at index `1` and the last item, as you see in the first two lines.

Another great feature in Swift is using ranges, which we used for replacing the items in the range from 0-2. This replaces the first three items with an empty array. That means the first three items have been removed. You can also replace it with an array containing data. Now, replace the items in the range with the items in the array. The most important thing is to be careful with the ranges that are used, and make sure that they are an inbound of the array. The out of bound ranges will throw exceptions.

Dictionaries

Dictionaries in Swift are like arrays in special characteristics, such as mutable and strongly typed. Dictionary is mutable by default, except if used with `let`. Also keys and values should be of the same type.

The dictionary type is inferred by the initial values, or you can explicitly write it using the square brackets `[keyType, valueType]`.

Initializing a dictionary

To initialize a dictionary, you have two options. The first option is to create an empty one with no data. You can create it like this:

```
var dic1 = [String:Int]() // 0 key/value pairs
```

As we see in this case, we had to explicitly write the type of keys and values.

In the second option, you have the predefined values like this:

```
var dic2 = ["EN" : "English", "FR" : "French"]
//["EN": "English", "FR": "French"]
```

Here we didn't write the type of keys or the values, as it was inferred from the initial values.

Appending or updating values

Updating or appending a value with a key in a dictionary is very similar, and can be done like this:

```
dic2["AR"] = "Arabic" //Add
dic2["EN"] = "ENGLISH" //update
//["EN": "ENGLISH", "FR": "French", "AR": "Arabic"]
```

As you can see, in the first line it will create a new record in the dictionary, because the "AR" key did not exist before. In the second line as the "EN" key exists, it will update each of its values with the given one. Very simple right!

Another method to update a value for the key in the dictionary is to call `updateValue(val, forKey:)`. Take a look at the following example:

```
dic2.updateValue("ARABIC", forKey: "AR") //returns "Arabic"
//dic2 now is ["EN": "ENGLISH", "FR": "French", "AR": "ARABIC"]
```

As you see in the code, this method returns the old value after updating the new value. So, if you want to retrieve the old value after the update function is done, this method is the best choice.

Removing items from the dictionary

This is the same as updating values. You have two ways to remove items from dictionary. The first is to set the value of the key as `nil`, and the second is to call the `removeValueForKey(key)` method. This method also returns the old value before deleting it.

```
dic2["AR"] = nil
dic2.removeValueForKey("FR") //returns French
//["EN": "ENGLISH"]
dic2["FR"]   // Returns nil
```

Enum

Enumeration is a very useful concept that is used to group related values together and define a new type for them. You must be familiar with enumeration in Objective-C or in C. Swift added new flavors to enum, and made it more flexible and easy to use.

To create enum in Swift, use the `enum` keyword, and then you can list all the possible cases after the `case` keyword:

```
enum LevelDifficulty{
    case Easy
    case Medium
    case Hard
    case Advanced
}
```

In the preceding code, we defined the new type as `LevelDifficulty` to group the related values of difficulties together (`Easy`, `Medium`, `Hard`, and `Advanced`). To use this enum, you can easily create variables with the `LevelDifficulty` type:

```
var easyMode = LevelDifficulty.Easy
//Type is inferred as LevelDifficulty

var mode : LevelDifficulty
mode = .Hard
```

As we see in this example, there are various ways to create enum. In the second one, for the variable `mode`, we set the type first, and then gave it a value. To set the value of a variable, we use a . (dot) operator.

Using enumerations with the switch statement

Swift makes life easy with enum. We can see this in the following example:

```
var power :Int
switch mode
{
case .Easy:
    power = 20
case .Medium:
    power = 30
case .Hard:
    power = 50
case .Advanced:
    power = 90
}
```

Very easy, isn't it? But take care of some the very important notes in the switch statement while using it in Swift:

- It has to be exhaustive, which means that you have to cover all the possible values of enum, and list them as cases, or use the default case.

- Swift doesn't support fallthrough. Unlike other languages, Swift doesn't fall through the bottom of each switch case into the next one. The switch statement finishes its execution as soon as a switch case is matched without explicitly writing a break statement. For sure, this makes your code safer by avoiding the execution of more than one switch case, by forgetting to add a break statement!

Enumerations with associated values

Swift gives enumerations another flavor and a great feature. This enables you to store the additional information for each member value. These associated values can be any given type, and can also be different for each member value. If you feel confused, look at the next example:

```
enum MissionState{
    case Accomplished(Int)
    case Attempted(String, Int)
    case UnAttempted
}
```

In this enum, in the case of Accomplished, we provide an integer value for it, which will represent the number of stars earned in this mission. In the case of Attempted, we provide two values for it. One is the string that represents the most progress achieved, and the other is the integer value for the number of attempts. The last one is UnAttempted, where we don't have to provide any additional information.

So now, let's see how to use this type of enumerations:

```
var state = MissionState.Accomplished(3)
var attemptState = MissionState.Attempted("80%", 3)
```

It is very easy to use this type of enumeration in the switch statement:

```
switch attemptState
{
case .Accomplished(let stars):
    println("Mission accomplished with \(stars) stars")
case .Attempted(let progress, let count):
    println("Mission attempted \(count) times with most progress
    \(progress)")
case .UnAttempted:
    println("UnAttempted")
}
```

To use the associated values in enumerations, Swift gives you the ability to label or describe these different values. This will make your code more readable and easy to use. To recreate our previous enum with labels, use the following code:

```
enum MissionState{
    case Accomplished(stars:Int)
    case Attempted(missionProgress:String, attemptsCount:Int)
    case UnAttempted
}

var state = MissionState.Accomplished(stars:3)
var attemptState = MissionState.Attempted(missionProgress: "80%",
attemptsCount: 3)
```

You can see how the labels make the code very understandable and easier to read.

Functions

In Swift, it's very easy to create the functions using the `func` keyword, followed by the function name and parameters between the parentheses. Parentheses are required even if the function doesn't take parameters. So we will use parentheses without writing anything in between. For some other languages we need to use the `void` keyword for the function that doesn't take parameters. Parameters are comma separated and each one is combined with two items: the name and the type of parameters, separated by : (colon). Check this example of a simple function:

```
func sayHi(name:String)
{
    println("Hi \(name)")
}


sayHi("John") //Hi John
```

One of the great features that I love in Objective-C is that you can write a full description for each parameter in methods, which helps everyone, working in the project, to understand the code. The same is here in Swift; you can label parameters more easily. To do so, just type the name (description) before the parameter, or add # before the name of parameter, if the name is sufficient as a description and meaningful. Check these two examples:

```
func joinStrings(string1 str1:String, toString str2:String,
joinWith j:String)
{
    println(str1 + j + str2)
}

joinStrings(string1: "John", toString: "Smith", joinWith: ",")
//"John,Smith"

func joinStrings2(#string1:String, #toString:String, #glue:String)
{
    println(string1 + glue + toString)
}

joinStrings2(string1: "John", toString: "Deo",glue: "/") //"John/Deo"
```

As we saw in the first method, we wrote the description for each parameter, so that the code would be readable and understandable. In the second one, the parameter names were self-explained, and they needed no explanation. In such a case, we just added # before them, and then the compiler treated them as labels for parameters.

Like any function in any language, Swift may return results after the execution. Functions can return multiple values and not just a value like Objective-C, thanks to tuples! To do this, just write - > after the parentheses, and then add a tuple that describes the results:

```
func getMaxAndSum(arr:[Int]) -> (max:Int, sum:Int)
{
    var max = Int.min
    var sum = 0
    for num in arr{
        if num > max
        {
            max = num
        }
        sum += num
    }
    return(max, sum)
}

let result = getMaxAndSum([10, 20, 5])
result.max //20
result.sum //35
```

Closures

Think of closures as a piece of code or functionality to pass around in your code. Closures in Swift are very similar to blocks in C and Objective-C. Closures in Swift are the first class type and it is allowed to be returned or passed as a parameter. And as we will see, functions are just special instances of closures. The general formula for closures is like this:

```
{ (params) -> returnType in

    //statements
}
```

As you can see, we opened curly braces, and then we added the necessary parameters followed by the return type and the in keyword. Knowing this formula will help you a lot in using closures, and you will not feel any frustration using it.

This is an example of using closures in sorting the collection of data:

```
var nums = [10, 3, 20, 40, 1, 5, 11]
sorted(nums, { (number1, number2) -> Bool in
    return number1 > number2
})
//[40, 20, 11, 10, 5, 3, 1]
```

Here, the closure is used to identify the comparison result of any two numbers. As we saw, the closure takes two parameters and returns a Boolean, that is the result of the comparison.

Summary

In this chapter, we saw what Swift is, and how the code structure works. We saw its new features by using arrays, dictionaries, functions, and closures. We also learned how to use Playground to try any piece of code in Swift anytime, without creating a new project, or even compiling and building your project. At the end of this chapter, you have the basic skills to write Swift code. In the next chapter, we will talk about some advanced features in Swift, including casting and checking, protocols, delegation, generics, memory management, and much more. Stay tuned!

2
Advanced Swift

Now, you have got some experience in the Swift programming language and have seen how funny and easy to learn it is. In this chapter, we will take you to the next level in Swift. We will talk about more advanced topics in Swift. For sure, we can't cover all topics in Swift, but we selected the most important and commonly used ones.

Type casting and type checking

Type casting and checking are ways used in Swift to check the type of instances and cast them to any different type. In Swift, we use as and is to perform type casting and type checking. Before going deep into how to use these operators, let's build an array that we will use in next examples:

```
var subViews = [UILabel(), UIButton(), UILabel(), UITextField(),
UITextView()]
```

We created an array of UI controls, but you might question, "how did you create array of objects of different types in Swift when you told us that Swift array is typed?" My answer is yes, you are right, but the Swift compiler is smart enough to check the items of the array; if they are different in type, it will search for the common superclass for them, which is UIView. So, this array is of type UIView.

Now, let's see how to check the type of items of this array. We will use the is operator followed by class name. Check the following code:

```
var labelsCount = 0
for view in subViews
{
    if view is UILabel
    {
        labelsCount++ // 2 times
    }
}
```

As we can see in the preceding code, we iterate through all the components in the array and find two labels based on the checking we made, using the `is` operator.

Downcasting

We saw how to check the type of an item, but what will happen if we want to use these items after checking? Imagine that we wanted to use the labels in the previous code; to do so, you have to downcast it to `UILabel` so that you can access attributes or methods specified for the `UILabel` class. In downcasting, we have two operators `as` and `as?`. Use the `as` operator if you are sure that the downcasting will always succeed, because the `as` operator will trigger runtime error if the downcasting fails. Use the `as?` operator when you are not sure if the downcasting will succeed because it will return optional value, which means that you will receive `nil` if the downcasting failed. Let's check these examples:

```
for view in subViews
{
    if view is UILabel // (Method 1)
    {
        let label = view as UILabel
        label.text = "bla bla bla"
    }

    if let button = view as? UIButton // (Method 2)
    {
        button.titleLabel?.text = "button"
    }
}
```

As you have seen in the previous code, in method 1, we used the `as` operator because we are sure that the `view` variable will be `UILabel` after we have checked its type using the `is` operator. In method 2, we use the `as?` operator and the condition will be `true` only if the casting succeeds and gives a non `nil` value.

Using Any and AnyObject

According to our explanation in the previous section about type casting and type checking, Swift provides us with two general types to use if you don't want to specifically type the objects:

- `AnyObject`: This type is used to represent instances of class types only and its equivalent to `id` in Objective-C

- `Any`: This type is used to represent instances of any type like tuples, closures, and so on

These types are very useful, especially when you try to deal with Cocoa APIs, because, most of the time, you will receive an array of type AnyObject. As we know, Objective-C doesn't support a typed array. In these situations, you have to use the is, as, and as? operators of type casting and type checking to help you deal with Any and AnyObject types.

Let's see an example of using AnyObject:

```
var anyObjects = ["Str", 5, true, UILabel(), NSDateFormatter()]
anyObjects.append(11.5)
anyObjects.append([1, 2])
```

As we have seen in this strange array, it holds String, UILabel, and NSDateFormatter. That works because, as we said, the compiler will try to get its common superclass and it will end up with the AnyObject type.

But, what about array items like 5 and true, are they also objects? The answer is yes because Swift bridged all variables and data to Foundation objects so String will be bridged to NSString, and Int and Bool will be bridged to NSNumber. The common superclass in that case will be NSObject, which is equivalent to AnyObject in Swift.

Please note that AnyObject is like an ID in Objective-C, so you can call any defined (built-in) function in it without warnings, but it will give a runtime error, as this object doesn't respond to this function. Check the following example:

```
var obj : AnyObject
obj = "Hello Swift"
obj = true
obj.stringByReplacingOccurrencesOfString(" ", withString: ",")
```

In this example, the last line will crash your app and give a runtime error because, in this case, this object is of type Number not String, and Number doesn't response to this function. Before using AnyObject, I suggest that you use one of type checking and type casting methods, which are is, as, and as?, to check the type before calling functions. In real-life coding, we will not do something like this to change the type of an object, but this example was just for explanation.

Now, let's see how Any is different than AnyObject. Take a look at the following example:

```
var whatever = [Any]()
//You can add anything you can imagine in this array :)

whatever.append(5)          // Int
whatever.append(5.0)        // Double
```

```
whatever.append(false)                    // Boolean
whatever.append((404, "Not Found"))  // Tuple
whatever.append({ (str:String) -> String in
    return str.uppercaseString
})                                   //Closure
```

As we have seen in the previous example, an array of `Any` type can hold any type of data you can imagine, even tuples and closures.

Protocols

Protocols are one of the most important and commonly used methodologies in programming in iOS and OS X. In protocols, you can define a set of methods and properties that will be implemented by classes that will conform to these protocols. In protocols, you just describe things without any implementations. In Swift, classes are not the only ones that can conform to protocols, but also structures and enumerations can conform to protocols as well.

To create a protocol, just use the `protocol` keyword and then its name:

```
protocol SampleProtocol
{

}
```

Then, when types are going to conform to this protocol, add a colon (`:`) after the name of type and list the protocols separated by commas (`,`). Check the following example:

```
class SampleClass: SampleProtocol, AnotherProtocol {

}
```

Now, let's talk about protocol properties and methods.

Properties

When you list properties between { } in protocol, you specify that these properties are required to exist in types that conform to this protocol. You define the property name and its type and whether this property is gettable or gettable and settable. In gettable properties, it means that instances can't set or change its value (read-only). To do this, type {get} after property declaration. In settable and gettable properties, instances are free to set and get its value. To do this, you can type {get set} after property declaration.

Let's see an example:

```
protocol VehicleProtocol
{
    var canFly:Bool {get} //Readonly
    var model:String {get set}
}

class Bicycle:VehicleProtocol
{
    var canFly:Bool
    {
        return false
    }
    var model:String = ""
}

var b1 = Bicycle()
b1.model = "model1"
b1.canFly
//b1.canFly = true   //Compile error
```

As you have seen in previous protocol, we defined two types of properties: read-only and settable one. The `Bicycle` class conforms to the protocol, so it has to define the properties that are defined in the `VehicleProtocol` protocol with the same property name and type. We set the value of the read-only `canFly` property in class declarations where instances can't change it. You will receive a compile error if you try to set this variable.

Methods

In a protocol, you can write methods to be implemented via types that will conform to this protocol. You can write the method name, return type, and parameters. Just write the signature of the method; there is no need to type { } or any implementation. Check the following examples:

```
protocol VehicleProtocol
{
    func move()
    func fullDistance() -> Double
}

class Bicycle:VehicleProtocol
{
```

```
    func move() {
        println("move logic goes here")
    }
    func fullDistance() -> Double {
        return 0.0
    }
}

var b1 = Bicycle()
b1.move() // prints: "move logic goes here"
```

As we mentioned earlier, structures and enumerations can conform to protocols; you can mark a method in protocol as mutating, which means that this method is allowed to modify the instance itself. That's possible because structures and enumerations are value types not reference types like classes.

To do so, just add the mutating keyword before the func keyword in declaring the method in the protocol. Then, you can simply implement it and modify the instance easily. Check the following example:

```
protocol Toggable{
    mutating func toggle()
}

enum Switch : Toggable{
    case ON
    case OFF
    mutating func toggle() {

        if self == ON
        {
            self = OFF
        }
        else
        {
            self = ON
        }
    }
}

var switch1 = Switch.OFF
switch1.toggle() //will be ON
```

As we have seen in the previous example, the mutating keyword tells the compiler that this method is capable of modifying the instance of value types. In implementation, we changed self to ON or OFF based on the current state of the instance value.

Class-only protocols

As classes, structures, and enumerations can adopt protocols, you can limit the conformance to classes only by marking the protocol as a class-only protocol. This can be done by adding the class keyword after the colon symbol (:) after the protocol name. Check the following example:

```
protocol classOnlyProtocol :class
{

}
```

Only classes can adopt this protocol. If you try to conform to this protocol with enumerations or structures, it will give you a compile-time error.

Protocol compositions

Once you create a protocol, you can use it as a type. This means that you can use it as a return type or parameter type in methods, as a type on variables and constants, and as a type for arrays or dictionaries.

When you use the protocol as a type, it can be used with multiple protocols using this form:

```
Protocol <protocol1, protocol2,…>
```

Let's check an example of using protocol as a type:

```
func registerVehicle(vehicle: protocol<VehicleProtocol,
VehicleInfo>)
{
    println("Description :\(vehicle.fullDescription())
            Distance:\(vehicle.fullDistance())")
}
```

As you can see in the previous function, it takes a parameter of type protocol that is composed of two protocols. That means that this method should take a type (class, enum, or struct) that conforms to both the VehicleProtocol and VehicleInfo protocols.

The protocol conformance

While classes, enumerations, and structures can conform to multiple protocols, sometimes, you may need to check for protocol conformance or cast to a specific protocol. We will use the same operators that we used in type checking and type casting, which are is, as, and as?. Let's use VehicleProtocol to build an example to check for protocol conformance:

```
class Bus: VehicleProtocol {
    func move() {

    }
    func fullDistance() -> Double {
        return 0.0
    }
    var canFly:Bool
        {
            return false
    }

    var model = "MM"
}


class Animal
{

}
class Bicycle:VehicleProtocol
{
    func move() {
        println("move logic goes here")
    }
    func fullDistance() -> Double {
        return 0.0
    }
    var canFly:Bool
    {
        return false
    }
    var model:String = ""
}

var objects = [Bus(), Bicycle(), Animal()]
for obj in objects
```

```
{
    if let vehicle =  obj as? VehicleProtocol
    {
        println("\(vehicle.model)")
    }
    else
    {
        //not vehicle
    }
}
```

As we can see in the example, we created another class Bus that conforms to VehicleProtocol. We also created another class Animal that doesn't conform to any protocol. Then, we created an array of different objects; some of them are vehicles (conform to VehicleProtocol) and others don't. We iterated over the array and used as? to cast VehicleProtocol if the casting succeed.

The optional requirements

Once you declare methods and properties in protocol, you are required to implement them in the type that will conform to this protocol. In some cases, you will find that some methods are not important for you to implement when you conform to some protocols.

In that case, Swift gives you the option to mark methods and attributes as optional by prefixing them with the keyword optional, so you don't have to implement such attributes or methods.

To add optional requirements, protocols should be marked with the @objc attribute. This attribute is written before the protocol keyword. This attribute indicates that the protocol should be exposed to Objective-C code (check working with Swift and Objective-C in a single project section for further information), and can be adopted only by classes and not by structures or enumerations. Once you add optional attributes and methods, they will return optional values when you call them. So, if they are not implemented and you call them, you will get the nil value. Let's check an example:

```
@objc protocol TableDataSource{

    func numberOfRows(#section:Int) -> Int
    optional func numberOfSections() -> Int
}

@objc class ViewController: TableDataSource
{
```

```
    func numberOfRows(#section: Int) -> Int {
        return 5
    }
}
```

In the previous code, we created a protocol with optional methods, and as you see, we marked it as @objc. When we implemented the TableDataSource protocol, we didn't implement the optional method numberOfSections() as it is marked optional.

Delegation

Delegation is the most commonly used design pattern in iOS. In delegation, you enable types to delegate some of its responsibilities or functions to another instance of another type. To create this design pattern, we use protocols that will contain the list of responsibilities or functions to be delegated. We usually use delegation when we want to respond to actions or retrieve or get information from other sources without needing to know the type of these sources, except that they conform to the protocol.

A good example to explain delegation is when you use UITableView. The table view can be used anywhere you want, and you can add it as subview in any part in your app. To enable the table to work properly, it needs some information, such as the number of cells and the cell that will be displayed, before displaying cells. It also needs to know which actions were performed, such as selecting cells. In that case, the table view has two properties called delegate and dataSource. They are protocols, and the table deals with them when it needs to obtain any information. It doesn't need to know the type of components that use it or the type of dataSource. They just have to conform to the UITableViewDelegate and UITableViewDatasource protocols. Let's check the implementation of delegate and dataSource of UITableView:

```
unowned(unsafe)var dataSource: UITableViewDataSource?
unowned(unsafe)var delegate: UITableViewDelegate?
```

As you can see, they are defined as protocols, so when any class wants to use it, it has to be the delegate and dataSource protocol of this table.

Another thing that I want to mention is that it's very common to mark the delegate property as optional and unowned. The unowned property will help in memory management, and we will talk about it in detail in the further sections. The delegate property will also help to have a default value as nil if you don't set the delegate. This will help in situations when you call methods in delegate and if the delegate property is not set yet; in that case, your app will not crash because you sent a message with the nil value.

Extensions

Extensions are used to add new functionality to an existing class, enumeration, or structure. They are like categories in Objective-C, but in Swift we have two differences:

- Extensions can be used with classes, enumerations, and structures
- Extensions don't have names

In Swift, extensions can do many things. Check this list:

- Add computed properties and computed type properties
- Add instance methods and class methods
- Define subscripts
- Add new initializers
- Make the existing type conform to protocol

To create an extension, use this form:

```
extension someType{
    //New functionalities go here
}
```

In extensions, as we said, you can add new functionalities, but you can't override an existing one.

Adding computed properties

Extensions can add computer instance properties and computed type properties in any existing type. Check the following example:

```
extension Double{

    var km : Double{
        return self / 1000.0;
    }
    var cm : Double{
        return self * 100.0
    }
}

var distance = 1500.0 // in meters
var distanceInKM = distance.km //1.5
var distanceInCM = distance.cm //150000
```

As we can see, we add two computed properties to the `Double` structure. The `km` property will be calculated by dividing the double value by 1000 and the same calculation is done for `cm` however it will be divided by 100. It will make your code readable, allowing you to just call the properties, and it will compute the result for you.

Adding new initializers

In extensions, you can add the new `init` method to an existing type. That will allow your type to have many options that can be be initialized, and will make your code more readable and usable. In the example, we will add a new initializer method to the `CGRect` structure. The `CGRect` structure has many `init` methods, but doesn't have one to be initialized using the `center` point, `width`, and `height`. Let's use extensions to add this new initializer to `CGRect`:

```
extension CGRect
{
    init(center:CGPoint, size:CGSize){

        let origin = CGPoint(x: center.x - size.width / 2, y:
        center.y - size.height / 2)
        self.init(x: origin.x, y: origin.y, width: size.width,
        height: size.height)
    }
}

let rect = CGRect(center: CGPoint(x: 50, y: 50), size:
CGSize(width: 20, height: 40))
//{x 40 y 30 w 20 h 40}
```

In the previous code, we added a new initializer to `CGRect` that accepts the `center` point and `size`. Then, we used `center` and `size` to get the `origin` point. We then used the built-in initializer that accepts `x`, `y`, `width`, and `height`.

Adding methods

In extensions, you can add instance methods and type methods to any existing type. You can call these new methods easily anywhere in your code. Let's see an awesome example in extending the `Int` type to contain a method that executes a piece of code repeatedly with integer value times. Check the example:

```
extension Int{
    func repeatTask(task:()->()){
        for _ in 0...self
            {
```

```
            task()
        }
    }
}

5.repeatTask{
    println("Hello Swift")
}
```

In the previous code, we added a new method called `repeatTask` that accepts closure with the format `() -> ()`, which means that it takes no parameters and returns nothing. It just executes the piece of code inside it. This method will run this closure integer X times. According to our example, we called the method toward the integer 5 with closure containing a single line of code to print message. This code will print `Hello Swift` five times.

The instance methods we add in extensions have the ability to modify (mutate) the instance itself. This can happen with value types only, which are enumerations and structures. To allow the method to do so, mark it as the `mutating` keyword before the `func` keyword while defining your function. Let's see an example in the `Int` structure:

```
extension Int{
    mutating func squareMe(){
        self = self * self
    }
    mutating func doubleMe(){
        self  = self * 2
    }
}

Var number = 10
number.squareMe() // number will be 100
number.doubleMe() // number will be 200
```

In the example, we added two mutating methods to the `Int` structure. The first one is called `squareMe` that will square the integer value itself. The second one is called `doubleMe` which doubles the integer value by multiplying it by 2. The two methods changed the integer value and mutated the instance.

Generics

The generic code is used to write usable and flexible functionalities that can deal with any type. This helps you avoid duplication and write code that is very clean and easy to edit and debug. Examples of using generics are when you use `Array` and `Dictionary`. You can create an array of `Int` or `String` or any type you want. That's because `Array` is generic and can deal with any type. Swift gives you the ability to write generic code very easily, as you will see in the following example. In the example, we will explain how to use Stack data structure. Stack is commonly used in algorithms and data structures. You can notice the use of stack in `UINavigationController`, as the view controllers are inserted in a stack, and you can easily push or pop view controllers.

Before implementing stack in a generic way, we will build it first for the `Int` type only, and then we will build it generically to see the difference. Check the following code:

```
class StackInt{
    var elements = [Int]()

    func push(element:Int)
    {
        self.elements.append(element)
    }
    func pop() -> Int
    {
        return self.elements.removeLast()
    }
    func isEmpty()->Bool
    {
        return self.elements.isEmpty
    }
}

var stack1 = StackInt()
stack1.push(5)     // Stack is [5]
stack1.push(10)   // Stack is [5,10]
stack1.push(20)  // Stack is [5,10,20]
stack1.pop()     // returns 20 and stack is [5, 10]
```

As we have seen in the previous code, we built a stack class to deal with the Int type elements. The code is simple and works great, but what about if we wanted to create another stack to deal with the String type or UIViewController type? For sure, we will not create another class for each type. The solution is to create a stack that deals with a generic type. Check how to do that in Swift:

```
class Stack <T>{
    var elements = [T]()
    func push(element:T)
    {
        self.elements.append(element)
    }
    func pop()->T{
        return self.elements.removeLast()
    }
}

var stackOfStrings = Stack<String>()
stackOfStrings.push("str1")
stackOfStrings.push("str2")

var stackOfInt = Stack<Int>()
stackOfInt.push(4)
stackOfInt.push(7)
```

As we have seen in the previous generic way, we created a stack class and wrote <T> to indicate that this class deals with generic type. Then in later functions, refer to the generic type with the T symbol, which means any type. After we created the stack data structure, we implemented the most important methods such as pop and push. We used it first with the String type and then with the Int type. Without modifying anything, we wrote the type while declaring the stack variable using the Stack<String>() way.

Operator functions

Operator functions or operator overloading is a way to allow structures and classes to provide their own implementation of existing operators. Imagine that you have two points of type CGPoint and you want to get the sum of both points. The solution will be to create another point and set its *x*, *y* with sum of *x*'s and *y*'s of points. It's simple right? But what if we override the + operator that accepts the summation of two points. Still not clear? Check this example:

```
func +(lhs:CGPoint, rhs:CGPoint) -> CGPoint
{
    return CGPoint(x: lhs.x + rhs.x, y: lhs.y + rhs.y)
```

```
        }

    let p1 =    CGPoint(x:  1,  y:  4)
    let p2 =    CGPoint(x:  5,  y:  2)

    let p3 = p1 + p2 //{x 6 y 6}
```

In the example, we wrote the function and its name is just the + operator. It takes two parameters, `lhs` and `rhs`, which means the left-hand side and right-hand side of the equation is a summation. The function returns a point, which is the sum of the two points. Then, in the code, we wrote `p1 + p2`. This code will call the + function that accepts two points and returns their sum. It makes your code very clean and readable.

Let's now override the subtraction operator -:

```
    func -(lhs:CGPoint, rhs:CGPoint) -> CGPoint
    {
        return CGPoint(x: lhs.x - rhs.x, y: lhs.y - rhs.y)
    }


    let p1 =    CGPoint(x:  1,  y:  4)
    let p2 =    CGPoint(x:  5,  y:  2)
    let p4 = p2 - p1  //{x 4 y -2}
```

It's very straightforward and done in the same way of addition. Let's now see more interesting operators like unary operators. The unary operators are used with a single target for example `i++`, `-a`, or `j--`. When you override operators like these, you type the `prefix` or `postfix` keyword before `func`, depending on whether the operators are coming after or before the operand. So, if you want to override `-a`, you use `prefix`, and for `i++`, use `postfix`. Now, let's implement the operators `-a` and `a++` for `CGPoint`:

```
    prefix func -(point:CGPoint) -> CGPoint
    {
        return CGPoint(x: -point.x, y: -point.y)
    }

    postfix func ++(point:CGPoint) -> CGPoint
    {
        return CGPoint(x: point.x + 1, y: point.y + 1)
    }
```

```
let p1 =  CGPoint(x: 1, y: 4)
let p11 = -p1 //{x -1 y -4}

let p22 = p1++ //{x 2 y 5}
```

As we can see in the examples, we override the two operators, - and ++. The two functions take only one parameter, as they are unary operators.

Other types of operators that I want to mention are compound operators, such as += and -=. In these types of operators, we create a function that takes two parameters, lhs and rhs, and then we mark the lhs parameter with the inout keyword to indicate that this parameter will be modified directly and that there is no need to return anything in this function. Let's see an example so that things will be clear:

```
func +=(inout lhs:CGPoint, rhs:CGPoint)
{
    lhs = lhs + rhs
}

let p1 =  CGPoint(x: 1, y: 4)
var p2 =  CGPoint(x: 5, y: 2)

p2 += p1 //{x 6 y 6}
```

When we implemented the += operators, we marked lhs with inout, and that helped us change the value directly without any need to return any values.

You can also override equivalence operators, such as == or !=, and you can add your custom operators such as +++ or ---. You can try it yourself as a test.

Memory management

Memory management is one of the most important topics that every developer should be aware of when making their app very responsive and efficient. Swift uses **Automatic Reference Counting (ARC)** to manage memory. In ARC, freeing up memory and managing it is done automatically when instances are no longer needed. Although ARC does most of the work in memory management, you have to care about the relations between classes to avoid memory leaks.

In memory, each object has a reference counting, and when it reaches zero, this object will be deallocated from the memory. In Swift, we have two types of references: strong and weak. The strong references retain the object and increment its reference counting by 1; the weak references don't increment the reference counting. In Swift, when you assign a class reference to a variable, constant, or a property, it makes a strong reference to it and it will remain in the memory as long as you use it. Take care while using relations between classes to avoid a very common problem-**Strong Reference Cycle**. This cycle happens when two instances hold the strong references to each other. Let's see an example of how this can happen:

```swift
class Person{
    var name:String
    var apartment:Apartment?
    init(name:String){
        self.name = name
    }
}

class Apartment {
    var apartmentNo:Int
    var owner:Person?
    init(number:Int){
        self.apartmentNo = number
    }
}

let person1        = Person(name: "John")
let apartment      = Apartment(number: 100)
person1.apartment  = apartment
apartment.owner    = person1
```

As we can see in the declarations of two classes, in the Person class we defined the property apartment to the Apartment class, which is strong. In Apartment, we have also assigned a property to the Person class, which is also strong. Then, in the example, we created two instances and assigned the properties to each other. The code looks good, but unfortunately, we made a big mistake here. Imagine that you have two dogs, and each one is attached to the other with a leash, so neither one can escape! It's the same case here; both the objects will be allocated in memory, and neither of them will be deallocated as each one of them is waiting for the other to destroy the first. The solution for this is to define one of the properties as weak or unowned. Check the differences and similarities between weak and unowned:

Weak	Unowned
• It doesn't keep the `strong` reference to instances. • Its default value is `nil` and it is set to `nil` when the referenced instance is deallocated. • Use it with the optional delegate.	• It doesn't keep the `strong` reference to instances. • It becomes a dangling pointer when the referenced instance is deallocated. Accessing a dangling pointer may crash your app. • It is always assumed to have a value. • It is similar to `assign` in Obj-C.

So, to solve our problem, we will redefine the `owner` property to be `weak`:

```
weak var owner:Person?
```

This will cause the person to retain the apartment, but the apartment will not retain the person. This relation is called the parent–child relation: the parent has to retain the child, but not vice versa - the child must not retain the parent. This means that the child should always exist while the parent exists, but the child doesn't have to exist if the parent doesn't exist. That's why we define the child to parent relation as `weak` or `unowned`. So, take care when you define relations between classes and understand when to use `strong`, `weak`, or `unowned`.

Using Objective-C and Swift in a single project

As an iOS developer, before Apple released Swift, you may feel worried about your old code in Objective-C and wonder if you can use them together. The answer is yes, you can use Swift and Objective-C together in a single project, and everything will be fine, irrespective of whether the project was originally in Swift or Objective-C. This compatibility is very important in making the language easy to use and has been welcomed by all developers. So, you can use Objective-C frameworks (system frameworks or your custom frameworks) in Swift, and you can use Swift API's in Objective-C code.

Importing Objective-C in the Swift project

To import some of your old Objective-C files in the Swift project, you will need a bridging header file to expose these files to Swift. Xcode offers to create the bridging header file for you once you add a Swift file in an Objective-C project or vice versa. Check the following image, where Xcode asks you to create the header file for you:

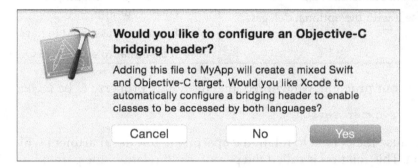

After clicking on **Yes**, Xcode will create a header file with the product name, followed by -Bridging-Header.h. In this file, you can import every Objective-C file you want to expose to Swift. Then, all Objective-C file's functionality will be available to use in any Swift file in your project without needing to import anything.

Importing Swift in the Objective-C project

To import Swift files in the Objective-C project, you will need Xcode-generated header file to expose these files to Objective-C. Xcode generates an Objective-C header file that declares Swift interfaces. The name of this file is the product name followed by Swift.h. Then, you can import this file in your Objective-C file as follows:

```
#import "ProductModuleName-Swift.h"
```

Limitations

Although the compatibility in using Objective-C and Swift in one project is important and mandatory, there are some limitations in using them together. Swift has some awesome new features, but unfortunately, most of them will not be usable in Objective-C. The following list shows the features that *can't* be used in Objective-C code:

- Generics
- Tuples
- Enumerations defined in Swift

- Structures defined in Swift

- Top-level functions defined in Swift

- Global variables defined in Swift

- Type aliases defined in Swift

- Swift-style variadic parameter

- Nested types

- Curried functions

Summary

In this chapter, we talked about some advanced features of Swift-like type casting and type checking. We talked about protocols and saw how Swift added some awesome new features to it than Objective-C. We also talked about extensions to add more usable and powerful functionality to any existing classes, structures, and enumerations. We introduced the operator overloading feature and generics to write more usable code. Finally, we talked about memory management to make your app more efficient and more responsive. We ended the chapter with how to use Swift and Objective-C together in the same project and listed the limitations of using some Swift features that can't be used in Objective-C.

Starting with the next chapter, we will mention a new technology in each chapter and how to write a simple demo in Swift. In the next chapter, we will talk about Touch ID, a new framework used to add a new flavor of authentication via finger print sensors.

3
Touch ID

Starting with this chapter, I will not talk only about Swift. However, I will talk about using Swift in developing apps with the new frameworks and tools introduced by Apple starting with iOS8 such as Touch ID, HealthKit, Metal, WatchKit, and app extensions. These awesome new tools let you write and add new features to your app or come with new app ideas.

What is Touch ID?

Touch ID is a new technology used for authentication starting with iOS 7 and iPhone 5s devices. Initially, it was used only by Apple to unlock the iPhone or make purchases through the App store. Developers couldn't use this technology in their apps. Starting with iOS 8, Apple has introduced a lot of new technologies, and one of them was using Touch ID in third-party apps. In that case, users can sign in to the apps using their fingerprints, and there is no need to enter a password! So, you can make the users life easier and simpler using this technology.

The LocalAuthentication framework

To start using Touch ID in your app, you have to use a new framework named **LocalAuthentication**. This framework provides everything you need to add Touch ID authentication in to your app. The framework is responsible for displaying the touch prompt to a user to provide his fingerprint for scanning to perform authentication. Some users may refuse to use it. If the authentication failed for any reason, in that case, you have to provide your own way for authentication like the old ways via e-mail or something else. Now, I will show you how to use the LocalAuthentication framework to prompt the user to authenticate himself.

The final result of our demo will be as follows:

The first step is to create a new iOS project with a single-view template and make sure that you select Swift as your development language. Then add LocalAuthentication framework, as follows:

Now that your project is configured to use Touch ID, open `ViewController.swift` and let's add a method called `authUser()` that will be used for authentication:

```swift
func authUser()
  {
      let context = LAContext()
      var authError : NSError?
      let reason = "Here explain why your app needs this
        authentication"

      if context.canEvaluatePolicy
      (LAPolicy.DeviceOwnerAuthenticationWith
      Biometrics, error: &authError)
      {
          //(1)
      }
          else{
          //(2)
      }
  }
```

In the previous code, we first created an authentication context that's represented by the `LAContext` class; the prefix **LA** is an abbreviation for **LocalAuthentication**. Then, we created an error variable `authError`; it will be set with an error that can occur in evaluating the authentication policy. The `reason` string holds the description that will appear to the user when the alert appears asking for the Touch ID. Before authentication, we have to make sure that the context can evaluate the `DeviceOwnerAuthenticationWithBiometrics` policy - whether Touch ID can be used for authentication. If the system can evaluate the policy, the code in part 1 will be executed, and otherwise, the code in part 2 will executed. Let's start implementing part 2:

```swift
if let error = authError{
    switch error.code{
    case LAError.TouchIDNotAvailable.rawValue:
        println("TouchID is not available in this device")
    case LAError.TouchIDNotEnrolled.rawValue:
        println("Authentication could not start because Touch ID
          has no enrolled fingers Availability")
    default:
        println("\(error.localizedDescription)")

    }
}
```

Here, we have an error. This error will mostly occur because of two cases. First, if the device that you are using has no Touch ID; that happen with all devices launched before iPhone 5s. Second, if the Touch ID has no available enrolled fingers. We used the `LAError` enum that contains all possible errors that may occur while dealing with LocalAuthentication. Let's move to part 1:

```
context.evaluatePolicy(LAPolicy.DeviceOwnerAuthenticationWithBiome
trics, localizedReason: reason, reply: { (success, error) -> Void
in

    if success{
        println("User authenticated successfully")

    }else{
        println("\(error.localizedDescription)")
        switch error.code{

        case LAError.UserCancel.rawValue:
            println("User cancelled")
        case LAError.UserFallback.rawValue:
            println("User entered custom password")
        case LAError.SystemCancel.rawValue:
            println("System cancelled")
        default:
            println("Auth failed")
        }

        //User didn't authenticate successfully
    }
})
```

Here, we can evaluate that Touch ID is available, so now we can call the `evaluatePolicy` function. Calling this method will prompt the user to provide his fingerprint for authentication, and the `reason` text will be visible to the user to understand why this app needs his Touch ID.

 Note that your fingerprint data is protected and is never accessed by iOS or other apps.

This method has closure callback to tell you what the result of authentication is. If `success` is `true`, the user authentication is done correctly and the user is ready to use your app. If not, you have many different scenarios such as cancelation by the user or the system or the user preferred to enter a password. To handle all these cases, we will also use `LAError` enum that covers all the possible cases of errors.

If you decide to put Touch ID authentication into your app, it should not be the only way for authentication. You have to provide other options because not all users may like to use or even have this feature in their device.

Summary

In this simple chapter, we introduced Touch ID, how you can use it in third-party applications and how to make it one of your options to sign in your app or authenticate your users. We also talked about the LocalAuthentication framework that performs all the magic about Touch ID authentication, simplifying everything for you to use it. In the next chapter, we will talk about the HealthKit framework and how to use it in developing apps related to users' health data. You will also learn how to read and write data from the HealthKit store and how to deal with data units.

Introduction to HealthKit

4

Starting with iOS 8, many frameworks and new APIs have been introduced to build awesome apps with new ideas. In this chapter, we are going to introduce one of these new frameworks, which is **HealthKit**. We will see how to use it to communicate with the native Health app in your iOS device.

What is HealthKit?

HealthKit is a new API provided by iOS 8. It enables apps to read the user's health information using the native Health app in their devices. You can consider that the Health app is a user interface for the HealthKit store. Other apps can write data in the Health app, such as workouts results, or statistics, so that the user can access them. This helps users to find all the information about their health in one location. The health information is stored in a secure location, and the user is responsible for deciding which data can be shared with apps. In the Health app, users can view, add, delete, and manage all their health data, and can also edit all the permissions to the third-party apps. HealthKit can also work with fitness or health devices, and it can save data from Bluetooth heart rate monitors. If your device has an M7 motion processor, HealthKit can import the step count data to it. So, all the developers who care about health and fitness apps will need to work with this new API.

HealthKit limitations

There are some limitations that everybody needs to be aware of before deciding to work with HealthKit:

- The HealthKit framework is introduced in iOS 8.
- HealthKit and the Health app are not available for iPad.

- The HealthKit framework can't be used in the app extensions, such as **WatchKit.**

- You need permission to access every type of data in the Health app. For example, a user can let your app read the blood type info, and prevent it from reading the heart rate or the step count info.

- The HealthKit store is encrypted, and your app can't read data when the phone is locked. So, when your app runs in background, it may not be able to access the store. However, your app can still write data even if the phone is locked, as the data will be cached, and then saved when the phone is unlocked.

- Any app that uses the HealthKit framework must provide a privacy policy.

HealthKit privacy

Health information is very sensitive, and HealthKit gives its users full control over their data to decide which data is to be shared with the third-party apps, and which apps can share or use this data. Here, I will list some points to consider while working with HealthKit:

- Don't use the information that is gained from HealthKit for advertising or other similar services.

- You must not disclose any information gained to a third party without getting permission from the user. Even with permission, you can share this data only with those third parties that provide fitness or health services.

- You can't sell information gained from HealthKit to any other service or platform.

- You can share this information with a third party, for medical research, only if the user consents.

Getting started with HealthKit

To get started with HealthKit, we will create a demo that will teach you how to request permission from the user to access his data from the Health app, read and format this information to make it readable for the user, and write info in the Health app. Now, go to Xcode and create a new project with a single view template, and make sure that Swift is selected as the project language.

Configuring the Xcode project

To configure our project using HealthKit, you have to first enable the HealthKit capabilities. To do this, select your target on Xcode, and click on the **Capabilities** tab. Then, enable **HealthKit** in the list by switching it ON; check the following screenshot:

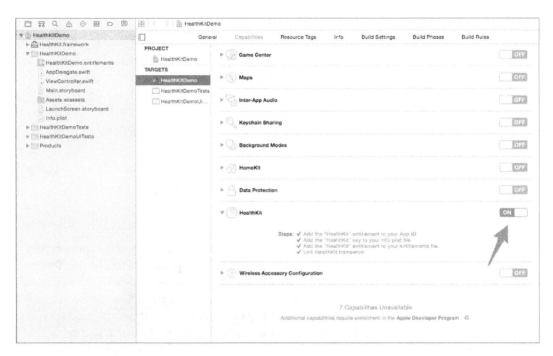

After enabling the HealthKit capabilities, HealthKit will be added to the list of required device capabilities. This will prevent users from installing your app on devices that don't support HealthKit, such as iPad. But what if HealthKit is not your main idea or the main operation in your app? In this case, you have to open the `info.plist` file of your app, and remove `healthkit` from the `Required device capabilities` array. Now, your project is ready to work with HealthKit.

Please make sure that your app identifier is set in a developer account, and you have enabled HealthKit on it. In the current example, I used Xcode 7, as Apple now allows developers to run apps on devices without the developer account, but you will have to login first with your iCloud account. So, if you use your developer account, please make sure that the HealthKit is enabled in the app identifier.

Getting your hands dirty with HealthKit

Now, we have configured our Xcode project. In the project demo, we will take permission for reading and writing information from HealthKit. We will ask for reading permissions to read age, weight, and height. Then, we will ask for writing permissions to write weight and height. Let's get started.

The HealthKit store

In your app, you need to instantiate a `HKHealthStore` object to be the interface between you and the HealthKit database. Once your app is launched, you need only one HealthKit store object per app; this is why we will declare it in `AppDelegate.swift`, and access it from all the view controllers or anywhere. Now, let's open `AppDelegate.swift` to import the HealthKit framework and define our store:

```
import UIKit
import HealthKit

let currentHealthStore = HKHealthStore()
```

As you see, after importing the HealthKit framework, we defined `currentHealthStore` to be our store, and we will access it anywhere in our project. Now, let's move to `ViewController.swift` to ask for the permission. Before this, we have to first check whether HealthKit is available in the current device or not. To do this, the `HKHealthStore` class has a class method called `isHealthDataAvailable` to tell you whether HealthKit is available in the current device or not. We do so because, as explained earlier, HealthKit is not available for iPad, and there are some specific editions of iPhone that also don't have HealthKit. Now, go to the `viewDidLoad` method in `ViewController.swift`, and check for the availability of HealthKit:

```
if HKHealthStore.isHealthDataAvailable(){
    // HealthKit is supported in this device

}
else{
    let alertController = UIAlertController(title:
    "Warning", message: "HealthKit is not available in
    your device!", preferredStyle:
    UIAlertControllerStyle.Alert)
    alertController.addAction(UIAlertAction(title: "Ok",
    style: UIAlertActionStyle.Cancel, handler: nil))
    self.presentViewController(alertController, animated:
    true, completion: nil)
}
```

As you saw in the previous code, we first checked for availability, and if it is not available, we displayed an alert to the user that HealthKit is not available in his or her device.

Asking for permissions

We have checked whether HealthKit is available or not. We will now ask for permission to read and write data. We will start with the data that we want to read. As we said before, we will read age, height, and weight. Let's create a method that returns all the types that we want to read:

```
func dataToRead() -> NSSet{
    let heightType =
    HKObjectType.quantityTypeForIdentifier
    (HKQuantityTypeIdentifierHeight)
    let weightType =
    HKObjectType.quantityTypeForIdentifier
    (HKQuantityTypeIdentifierBodyMass)

    let birthdateType =
    HKObjectType.characteristicTypeForIdentifier
    (HKCharacteristicTypeIdentifierDateOfBirth)

    return NSSet(objects: heightType!, weightType!,
    birthdateType!)

}
```

In the previous code, we created a method that returns the NSSet of objects. These objects will be the types that we want to read. In HealthKit, all types are the subclasses of the HKObjectType class, which has all the common functionalities and properties of all the subclasses. In the data that we read, we used two types of data: HKQuantityType and HKCharacteristicType. The HKQuantityType class is a subclass of HKObjectType, and is used for quantity types that are stored as numeric values. The HKCharacteristicType class is also a subclass of HKObjectType, and is used to represent data that doesn't change over time, such as sex or date of birth. The characteristic types cannot be used to create new HealthKit objects. Instead, users must enter and edit their characteristic data using the Health app. Characteristic types are used only when asking for permission to read data from the HealthKit store.

Let's now create a method to return data that we want to write:

```
func dataToWrite() -> NSSet{

    let heightType =
    HKObjectType.quantityTypeForIdentifier
    (HKQuantityTypeIdentifierHeight)
    let weightType =
    HKObjectType.quantityTypeForIdentifier
    (HKQuantityTypeIdentifierBodyMass)

    return NSSet(objects: heightType!, weightType!)
}
```

The data that we write will be same as the data we read, only without the date of birth, because it's a characteristic type, and can be changed only from the Health app.

Now that the types are ready, let's ask for permission to read and write this data. We will use `currentHealthStore` in `AppDelegate` to ask for authorization. Update the code in `viewDidLoad` to look like this:

```
if HKHealthStore.isHealthDataAvailable(){
        // HealthKit is supported in this device

        let typesToRead = dataToRead()
        let typesToWrite = dataToWrite()

        currentHealthStore.requestAuthorizationToShareTypes
        (typesToWrite as! Set<HKSampleType>, readTypes:
        typesToRead as! Set<HKObjectType>, completion: {
        (success, error) -> Void in

            if success{

                // We will update UI to preview data we read.
                dispatch_async(dispatch_get_main_queue(), { ()
                -> Void in

                    self.updateUI()
                })

            }
            else{
```

```
        print("User didn't allow HealthKit to access
        these read/write data types",
        appendNewLine:true)
    }

})
}
```

We started our authorization by calling the `requestAuthorizationToShareTypes` method, which takes the read and write types as the parameters to display a view to the user asking for permission. After the user responds to the request, the completion block will be called with success and error. If everything goes fine, the success variable will be true, and you can update your UI this time. Now, run your app in the device, and you will see something like this:

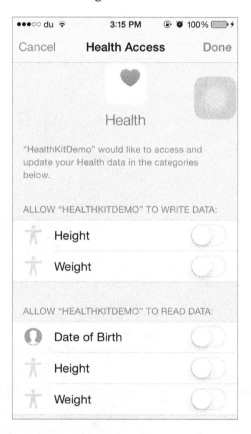

As you see, this view is displayed to ask the user to approve which data type we have access to. And as we said before, HealthKit gives users full control over which the data type can be accessed for read or write.

Updating the UI

Now, we can read and write the data types that the user has approved to access. We will now start to display the read data types. Let's first create a new view controller class with a subclass to `UITableViewController`, and it will be our `HomeViewController` class. Then move all the code we wrote in `ViewControlelr. swift`, to the new one that is `HomeViewController. swift`, as shown in the following screenshot:

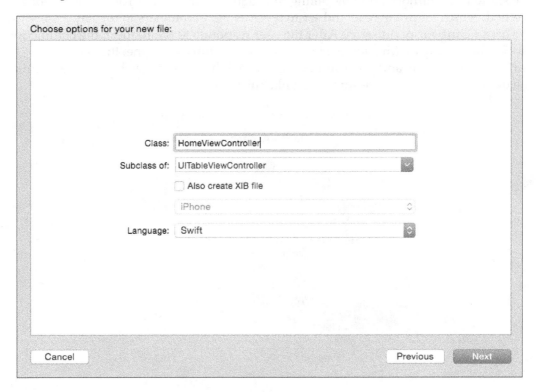

Now, switch to the `Main. storyboard` file to design the UI of `HomeViewController`. Now, from the right-hand side menu, drag `UITableViewController` and set its class to `HomeViewController`. Check out the following screenshot:

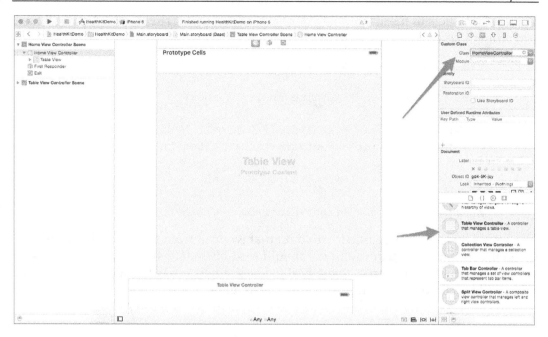

After adding `UITableViewController`, we will modify it to add the static cells that will display the information that we read from the HealthKit store. Now, select `UITableView` and change **Content** to `static cells`, and **Style** to `Grouped`. Then, add three cells to represent age, height, and weight. The design will be something like this:

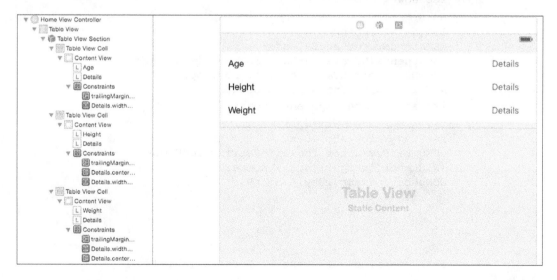

Then, take outlets to these labels in your `HomeViewController.swift`. You will have something like this:

```
@IBOutlet weak var ageLabel: UILabel!

@IBOutlet weak var ageValueLabel: UILabel!

@IBOutlet weak var heightLabel: UILabel!
@IBOutlet weak var heightValueLabel: UILabel!

@IBOutlet weak var weightLabel: UILabel!

@IBOutlet weak var weightValueLabel: UILabel!
```

Now, the UI is ready to be filled with data that we read from the HealthKit store. Open the `updateUI` function, and we should read birth date, height, and weight. We will read each type in a separate method to keep our code more readable. Let's start with the birth date by creating a function called `updateUsersAge()`:

```
func updateUsersAge(){

    do{
        var error : NSError!
        let birthdate = try
        currentHealthStore!.dateOfBirthWithError()

        let now = NSDate()

        let dateComponents =
        NSCalendar.currentCalendar().
        components(NSCalendarUnit.NSYearCalendarUnit,
        fromDate: birthdate, toDate: now, options:
        NSCalendarOptions.WrapComponents)
        let age = dateComponents.year

        self.ageValueLabel.text =
        NSNumberFormatter.localizedStringFromNumber
        (NSNumber(integer: age), numberStyle:
        NSNumberFormatterStyle.NoStyle)

    }
    catch{

        self.ageValueLabel.text = "Not Available"
    }
}
```

The code is straightforward — we used our store instance called currentHealthStore to call the dateOfBirthWithError() function, to get the user's data of birth from the Health app. The catch block will be called if there has been any error, or if the date of birth is not available in the store. Once you get the date of birth, you can use NSDateComponents and NSCalendar to get the difference of years to the current year. Then, update the UI by setting the text to the outlet label called ageValueLabel.

Now, let's see how to read height and weight. Before seeing how to read this data, I want to explain something. In HealthStore, when you read the quantity types, you run a query to fetch data, as this type has different values within the time. For example, in the previous year, if you have reported your weight in the Health app 10 times with different values, and then when you read the weight data from the store, you will have to specify which is the data that you need. In some apps, they may need to read the weight records of the previous year, only to display a chart about your progress in weight loss. In our app, we care only about the most recent value, which means your current weight. This is why, in reading the quantity types, you have to specify NSSortDescriptors, when you need to sort this data in any specific order. You can also specify NSPredicate if you want to filter the data; for example, read all the weights that are greater than 100 kg so that I will be able to know which times in the year I put on weight: in summer, or winter, or during school days. The last thing is that you can specify the limit that you want to read, for example, if you only care about the last five records you will set the limit value as 5. It makes the execution of the query faster if you don't need all the records, and care only about a specific number.

So, because we only care about the most recent value, let's first use the Swift feature of extensions to create an extension for HKHealthStore, to read the most recent value of a specific data type. Check out the following code:

```
typealias MostRecentCompletionHandler = (quantity:HKQuantity!,
error:NSError!) -> Void

extension HKHealthStore{

    func getMostRecentValueOfType(quantityType:HKQuantityType,
    predicate:NSPredicate, handler:MostRecentCompletionHandler){


        let sortDescriptor = NSSortDescriptor(key:
        HKSampleSortIdentifierEndDate, ascending: false)
        let query = HKSampleQuery(sampleType: quantityType,
        predicate: predicate, limit: 1, sortDescriptors:
        [sortDescriptor]) { (query, samples, error) -> Void in
```

```
        if let results = samples{

            let sample = results.first as! HKQuantitySample

            handler(quantity: sample.quantity, error: nil)

        }
        else{
            handler(quantity: nil, error: error)
        }

    }

    self.executeQuery(query)
  }
}
```

As we saw, in the previous extension, we created `NSSortDescriptor` to sort the quantities by the end date to get the most recent record. Then, we created `HKSampleQuery` object using four parameters; the quantity type that we want to read and its passed as a parameter in the `getMostRecentValueOfType` method, the sort descriptor which we have created earlier, the `NSPredicate` as a `nil` value because we don't want to filter records, the results limit with 1 value as we want to read only the most recent one, and finally the completion block that gives you with query, samples and error. After executing the query, the completion block will be called; inside the block we will call our handler that was passed also as a parameter in the `getMostRecentValueOfType` method with the first quantity and error if occurred. Now, let's go back to creating a function to read the height:

```
func updateUsersHeight(){

    self.heightLabel.text = "Height (m)"
    let heightType =
    HKQuantityType.quantityTypeForIdentifier
    (HKQuantityTypeIdentifierHeight)
    currentHealthStore.getMostRecentValueOfType(heightType!,
    predicate: nil, handler: { (quantity, error) -> Void in

        if quantity != nil{

            let mUnit = HKUnit.meterUnit()
            let height = quantity.doubleValueForUnit(mUnit)
```

```
dispatch_async(dispatch_get_main_queue(), { () ->
Void in

    self.heightValueLabel.text = "\(height)"
})
}
else{
dispatch_async(dispatch_get_main_queue(), { () ->
Void in

    self.heightValueLabel.text = "Not Available"
})
}
})
}
```

As we saw in the previous code, we called the getMostRecentValueOfType method that we added using the Swift extension. We passed the height type and the completion handler to get the quantity and error if occurred. The quantity will be nil if the user has not set his height in the Health app, and this is why we display the Not Available message. If the quantity is not nil, we format the value to be in a meter using the HKUnit class. HKUnit has many other units to use, such as inch or mile.

In the same way, we will now read the weight from the HealthKit store:

```
func updateUsersWeight(){
    self.weightLabel.text = "Weight (Kg)"
    let weightType =
    HKQuantityType.quantityTypeForIdentifier
    (HKQuantityTypeIdentifierBodyMass)
    currentHealthStore.getMostRecentValueOfType(weightType!,
    predicate: nil, handler: { (quantity, error) -> Void in

        if quantity != nil{

            let gUnit = HKUnit.gramUnit()
            let weight = quantity.doubleValueForUnit(gUnit) /
            1000.0
            dispatch_async(dispatch_get_main_queue(), { () ->
            Void in

                self.weightValueLabel.text = "\(weight)"
            })
        }
        else{
```

```
dispatch_async(dispatch_get_main_queue(), { () ->
Void in

    self.weightValueLabel.text = "Not Available"
})
    }
})
}
```

Now, update your `updateUI` method to be like this:

```
func updateUI(){

    updateUsersAge()
    updateUsersHeight()
    updateUsersWeight()
}
```

Now, if you run your app, you will see something like this:

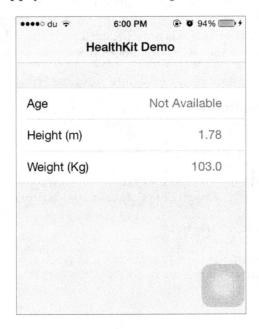

Sharing data in the Health app

We have learned how to ask for the permission, and read information from the Health store. Now we see an example of how to share data in Health store. In this example, when the user clicks on the weight row, a pop-up view will be displayed, where the user will have to enter his new weight. Then, the user can save this value in the HealthKit store. Let's start with the UI to detect click on table cells and display the pop-up view. To detect, click on `UITableViewCell`, we will add the `didSelectRowAtIndexPath` function, as follows:

```
override func tableView(tableView: UITableView,
didSelectRowAtIndexPath indexPath: NSIndexPath) {

    if indexPath.row == 2{
        //Weight cell

        let alertController = UIAlertController(title: "Your
        current weight", message: nil, preferredStyle:
        UIAlertControllerStyle.Alert)
        alertController.addTextFieldWithConfigurationHandler({
        (textField:UITextField) -> Void in
            textField.keyboardType = UIKeyboardType.DecimalPad
        })

        alertController.addAction(UIAlertAction(title: "Ok",
        style: UIAlertActionStyle.Default, handler: {
        (alertAction:UIAlertAction) -> Void in

            if let textField =
            alertController.textFields?.first {

                let value = (textField.text! as
                NSString).doubleValue
                self.saveWeightInStore(value)
            }


            tableView.deselectRowAtIndexPath(indexPath,
            animated: true)

        }))

        alertController.addAction(UIAlertAction(title:
        "Cancel", style: UIAlertActionStyle.Cancel, handler: {
        (alertAction) -> Void in
```

```
                    tableView.deselectRowAtIndexPath(indexPath,
                    animated: true)
            }))
            self.presentViewController(alertController, animated:
            true, completion: nil)
        }
    }
```

We checked first that the selected row is the weight row and then displayed `UIAlertController` with `UITextField` to enter the new height. When the user clicks on **OK**, we will take the new value and save it in HealthKit store using the function `saveWeightInStore(value)` that we will now implement.

Now that the new weight value is ready, let's implement the `saveWeightInStore(newValue)` function:

```
    func saveWeightInStore(weight:Double){

        let gramUnit = HKUnit.gramUnit()
        let quantity = HKQuantity(unit: gramUnit, doubleValue:
        weight * 1000.0)
        let weightType =
        HKQuantityType.quantityTypeForIdentifier
        (HKQuantityTypeIdentifierBodyMass)

        let now = NSDate()
        let sample = HKQuantitySample(type: weightType!, quantity:
        quantity, startDate: now, endDate: now)
        currentHealthStore.saveObject(sample) { (success, error) -
        > Void in

            if success{

                self.updateUsersWeight()
            }
            else{
                print("Error in saving \(error)")
            }
        }
    }
```

To save any data in the Health store, you have to prepare the HKQuantitySample instance that takes the quantityType parameter, which here is weightType. Then we also have the quantity type parameter which we created using the gram unit and the value. We multiplied the value by 1000.0 to convert it into grams. Then, we called the saveObject method in currentHealthStore, to save the data in store, and, if the saving operation succeeded, we refreshed the UI with the new value by calling the updateUsersWeight method.

Summary

In this chapter, we covered in detail how to get started with HealthKit. We explained the idea of the HealthKit framework, and how to deal with sensitive data. We mentioned the HealthKit limitations, and its availability in the iOS devices. We saw how the users' data is protected in the Health app, and any app that needs to access or share any data type will need permission from user. The user can enable or disable this permission anytime from the Health app. We also learned how to read and share the data to the Health store, and how to deal with units. In the next chapter, we will give a good introduction, and the basic information that is needed to get started with Metal. Metal is a new framework for the GPU-accelerated 3D graphics in iOS.

5

Introduction to Metal

We are still working with the new features of iOS 8, and in this chapter, we are going to talk about Metal. To work with graphics in mobile devices is not an easy task especially with complex graphics and 3D. Mobile devices are limited resources, and you have to care about your performance and battery usage. We used to use **OpenGL ES** or other high-level APIs such as **SceneKit**, but these tools don't give you full power and control to optimize performance. That's why Apple has come up with Metal, and they claimed that it's the lowest overhead access to the GPU.

What is Metal?

Metal is a new framework specified for GPU-accelerated advanced 3D graphics. Apple first introduced Metal in iOS 8. To work with Metal, you need a physical device as it's not supported yet in iOS simulator. The physical device must also have an Apple A7 or A8 processor or higher (at the moment there is no higher processor, but I have included it just in case Apple introduces A9 while you are reading this chapter). This means that you need an iPhone 5s or higher or an iPad Air or Mini (second generation) to run Metal.

Features

Metal has a lot of features that make it a good choice to use in your 3D graphics app or game. Here you can find a list of features of Metal:

- It provides extremely low-level access to A7 and A8 GPU to enable high performance to your graphics rendering.

- It eliminates a lot of performance bottlenecks, such as state validation, that is found in most common graphics APIs.

- It is designed to be efficient with Apple hardware to ensure the highest speed with low overhead.

- It provides up to 10x number of draw calls in your app compared to OpenGL ES.

- A big enhancement in game is load time performance, thanks to the support of precompiled shaders. They're an incredibly important part of rendering a realistic gaming experience. Precompiling enables them to load faster.

- It is designed to move all expensive operations and creation of objects to be outside the runtime of the game loop.

Although Metal is very efficient and gives you high performance, I really don't recommend it as a choice to make a 3D game. In Metal, you will write a lot of code to handle drawings of all your models and graphics, which is very time consuming and a big headache. Maybe big gaming companies will use it, but I think that they will build their own game engines based on Metal to make their life easier.

If you are working as an individual and looking forward to building your own game, go with SceneKit, Unity, or Unreal Engine. These game engines are very powerful, and incredible games have been published using them. You can also go with Metal and understand everything in it and how it works, and then try to build your own game engine. In this case, you will get an incredible experience in 3D graphics and game development.

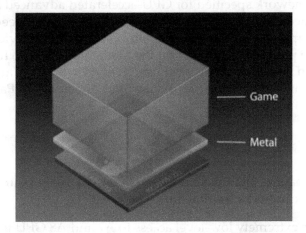

As we have seen in the previous image, Metal has extremely low-level access to A7 and A8 GPU to enable high performance to your graphics rendering

3D rendering

To render in 3D, you need to convert your 3D world to 2D images by applying effects and methods to make them look plausible. You take geometric data of your world and add perspective, material properties, lighting, and textures. Then, with some illusion and understanding of the human visual system, you make things look real.

Pipeline

In the past, we had the "fixed-function" pipeline, which means that the hardware is configurable, not programmable. So, you have to set certain states in the GPU to be applied. For example, in lighting or changing graphic states for textures, you can't write your own shaders. Then, the "programmable" pipeline that contains shaders was introduced. Shaders are small programs to be run per pixel or vertex. In that case, you write code that runs directly on the GPU. To make things clear, assume that we want to display a model on the screen. The object will be passed through the vertex shader, which projects this object on the virtual view plane. Then, the object will be chopped into pixels, which will be passed through a fragment shader to assign a color value for each pixel. So, to summarize, what happens in the draw call is that each pixel gets a position in 3D space (x, y, and z) and is labeled with a color (r, g, b, and a).

Transformations

Transformations are used for moving an object around the world. Examples for transformations are translation, rotation, and scaling. The perspective projection is also considered as a form of transformation and is the most commonly used in 3D rendering.

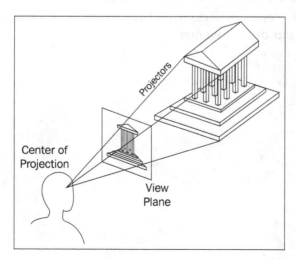

Projection

In the process of perspective projection, we go through many coordinate spaces. First, the points are represented in its own model space. Then, we need to move from the model space to the world space, and then to the eye space so that we can imagine the world from that space. In mathematics, we achieve this by matrix concatenation.

Other options to work with 3D rendering in iOS

As we said earlier, Metal is not the only option for you to work in 3D application or game. You have some other frameworks or third-party game engines, such as Unity or Unreal Engine. One of the built-in native frameworks is SceneKit. SceneKit is a very high-level engine that works with 3D models and worlds and can be used easily with SpriteKit. Both are high level, as we said, and don't give you any flexibility to work with low-level code or any access to GPU. For example, if you want to render a 3D model in SceneKit, it's just a piece of cake. But in Metal, it's not easy as it will take a lot of time and need a lot of code to be written. The trade-off is the full power and control while drawing this model. The other option is OpenGL ES, which is considered a great technology to work with 3D in iOS because of its high performance and the power it gives you during work - the same for its cross-platform. Metal gives you more power than OpenGL ES to interact with GPU. It also has control over everything; although it's not cross-platform, it's designed to work extremely efficient with Apple hardware.

Getting started with Metal

Now I think you have enough background knowledge to get started with Metal. Let's start building our demo together.

1. Open Xcode, create new project, and choose the **Game** template.

2. Then, write the name of the MetalDemo project, choose **Swift** as a language, and select **Metal** in the **Game Technology** options list.

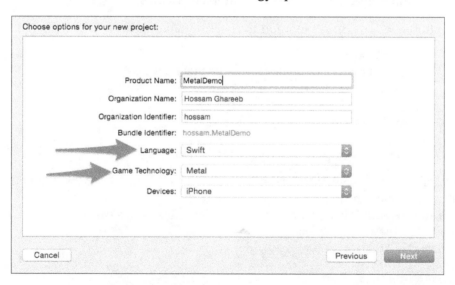

3. Now, build and run in your device. You should see a beautiful triangle moving in 3D.

We will go through the code together and explain the most important parts of it in how to draw this triangle.

Devices and CAMetalLayers

Open `GameViewController.swift`, and you will see that we have to first import Metal framework. Then, if you checked the first two attributes, you should see something like this:

```
let device = { MTLCreateSystemDefaultDevice() }()
let metalLayer = { CAMetalLayer() }()
```

Creating devices is considered the first step in your Metal code. Devices are the abstractions over GPU in your iOS device. Devices conform to protocol `MTLDevice`, and you can consider them as the heart of Metal because they're your direct connection to the GPU. Using devices, you can create pipelines, textures, and buffers.

The second important step in your work with Metal is creating `CAMetalLayer`. It is a subclass of `CALayer`, but with more capabilities and special effects. This layer is your UI interface and where you can see your Metal drawings.

Now, go to the `viewDidLoad` method to check some initialization:

```
metalLayer.device = device
metalLayer.pixelFormat = .BGRA8Unorm
metalLayer.framebufferOnly = true

self.resize()

view.layer.addSublayer(metalLayer)
```

We first tell `CMMetalLayer` which device to listen to. Then, we set the pixel format to `BGRA8Unorm`, which mean an 8-bit color format. Finally, we add `CMMetalLayer` as a sublayer to the main layer of the view controller `view`, so we can see the drawings on the screen.

Now, after we have created CMMetalLayer, we need to resize it and update its frame to meet the device screen size. Go and check a function called resize to set the layer frame:

```
func resize() {
        if (view.window == nil) {
            return
        }

        let window = view.window!
        let nativeScale = window.screen.nativeScale
        view.contentScaleFactor = nativeScale
        metalLayer.frame = view.layer.frame

        var drawableSize = view.bounds.size
        drawableSize.width = drawableSize.width *
        CGFloat(view.contentScaleFactor)
        drawableSize.height = drawableSize.height *
        CGFloat(view.contentScaleFactor)

        metalLayer.drawableSize = drawableSize
    }
```

As you can see, we first get the native device screen scale and the current drawable view size. Then, we set layer frame and its drawableSize variable, which is calculated by the view size multiplied by the scale of device screen. This method should be called only in the overridden viewDidLayoutSubviews method.

The command queue

In GameViewController.swift, you will find the declaration and creation of the command queue like this:

```
var commandQueue: MTLCommandQueue! = nil
// in viewDidLoad
commandQueue = device.newCommandQueue()
```

To submit work to the GPU, you need `MTLCommandQueue`, which conforms to the protocol `MTLCommandQueue`. This queue is just a serial queue that dispatches your work to the GPU. Submitting work in `MTLCommandQueue` is thread-safe, so you can submit work to it through multiple threads with no problem.

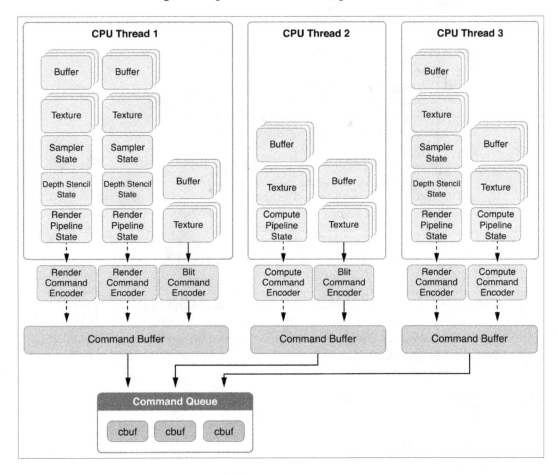

In the previous figure, we can see three threads are submitting work to the command queue in parallel, and each thread has its own command buffer.

Vertex and color buffers

Anything that can be drawn in Metal is decomposed into a series of triangles by stitching them together seamlessly and painting over them with textures. These two buffers indicate the vertices and colors used for drawing the triangle, and they are instances of MTLBuffer. In the list of parameters, you should see them declared like this:

```
var vertexBuffer: MTLBuffer! = nil
var vertexColorBuffer: MTLBuffer! = nil
```

Then, to create them, we will use the device that we created earlier:

```
let vertexColorSize = vertexData.count *
sizeofValue(vertexColorData[0])
        vertexColorBuffer =
        device.newBufferWithBytes(vertexColorData, length:
        vertexColorSize, options: nil)
```

The vertexData and vertexColorData are arrays of float declared in the top of your GameViewController.swift file. Then, we use the newBufferWithBytes instance method in the device to create the buffer.

Vertex and fragment shaders

Shaders are small programs or functions that run on the GPU. You can find a vertex shader and fragment shader created in the Shaders.metal file in your Xcode project. They are written in a language such as C++ called **Metal Shading Language**. The vertex shader is called once per vertex/pixel. It takes the vertex information (position and color) as a parameter and returns modified data for position and color. In Xcode, you can create multiple shaders in the same file or spread them across many metal files. Metal will load all the shaders added in any metal file in your project. Check the following figure to see the input of vertex function:

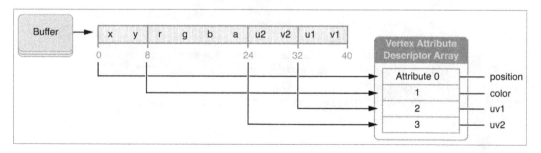

After the vertex shader has finished its work, its output will be considered as an input for the fragment shader. Then, it will also be called per vertex, and its job will be to return the final color of this vertex. If you checked the `Shaders.metal` file, you will find that it returns **half4**. It means a four-component color RGBA.

Now, to create these programs, check the `viewDidLoad` method. You will find something like this:

```
let defaultLibrary = device.newDefaultLibrary()
       let fragmentProgram =
       defaultLibrary?.newFunctionWithName("passThroughFragment")
       let vertexProgram =
       defaultLibrary?.newFunctionWithName("passThroughVertex")
```

Again, we will use our device to create an instance of `MTLLibrary` by calling `newDefaultLibrary()`. This library is a collection of functions that can be retrieved by name. The default library consists of all the shaders that have been compiled in your app binary.

The render pipeline

The render pipeline is considered as a precompiled set of graphic states, vertex shader, and fragment shader. We create the pipeline in the setup of your code and configure it with the vertex function and fragment function. The creation of pipelines is expensive because when you create them, they takes the shader code and compile it down to the GPU. That's why we create one in the setup and keep reference to its state:

```
let pipelineStateDescriptor = MTLRenderPipelineDescriptor()
       pipelineStateDescriptor.vertexFunction = vertexProgram
       pipelineStateDescriptor.fragmentFunction = fragmentProgram
       pipelineStateDescriptor.colorAttachments[0].pixelFormat =
       .BGRA8Unorm

       var pipelineError : NSError?
       pipelineState =
       device.newRenderPipelineStateWithDescriptor
       (pipelineStateDescriptor, error: &pipelineError)
       if (pipelineState == nil) {
           println("Failed to create pipeline state, error
           \(pipelineError)")
       }
```

As you see, the pipeline is an instance of `MTLRenderPipelineDescriptor`, and it is then configured with the vertex and shader programs that we mentioned in the previous section. Then, as usual, we will use the device to create `pipelineState`, which is a compiled pipeline configuration and is efficient to use.

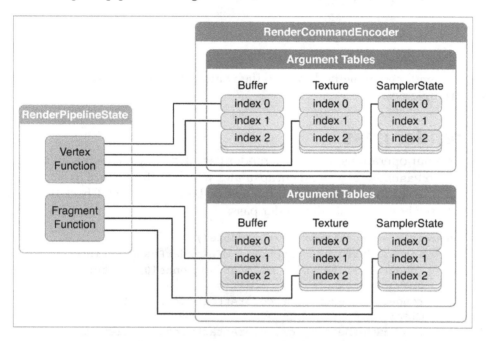

Vertex function and fragment function properties are essential for `MTLRenderPipeLineState`.

The game loop and rendering

Now we have configured everything, it is time to write the game loop to render and draw the triangle in each frame.

The display link

We need a function to be called every time when the device screen refreshes. To do that, we use an instance of the `CADisplayLink` object, which is a timer object that allows your application to synchronize its drawing to the refresh rate of the display. In the `viewDidLoad` method, you will find it created:

```
timer = CADisplayLink(target: self, selector:
Selector("renderLoop"))
        timer.addToRunLoop(NSRunLoop.mainRunLoop(), forMode:
        NSDefaultRunLoopMode)
```

Now, the timer is created and `GameViewController` is its target. The `renderLoop()` function will be called in each frame:

```
func renderLoop() {
        autoreleasepool {
            self.render()
        }
    }
```

Inside the `renderLoop` method, we call the `render` method in which we redraw the update triangle position.

The render pass

To perform our operations, we need a render pass descriptor, which is an instance of `MTLRenderPassDescriptor`. It encapsulates which buffer texture to be rendered and the clear color to be used to clear the texture before drawing. Check the `render` function to see how to create the render pass:

```
let drawable = metalLayer.nextDrawable()
        let renderPassDescriptor = MTLRenderPassDescriptor()
        renderPassDescriptor.colorAttachments[0].texture =
        drawable.texture
        renderPassDescriptor.colorAttachments[0].loadAction =
        .Clear
        renderPassDescriptor.colorAttachments[0].clearColor =
        MTLClearColor(red: 0.65, green: 0.65, blue: 0.65, alpha:
        1.0)
        renderPassDescriptor.colorAttachments[0].storeAction =
        .Store
```

As we can see in the code, `CAMetalLayer` that we created earlier can give you a `drawable` object that can give you a texture to draw into.

The command buffer

Do you remember the command queue that we talked about earlier to dispatch work to GPU? Now we will see the commands that will be submitted to that queue and be executed at this frame. Command buffers consist of encoded or rendered commands written by the command encoders. To create a render command, check this in the `render` function:

```
let commandBuffer = commandQueue.commandBuffer()
///
let renderEncoder =
commandBuffer.renderCommandEncoderWithDescriptor(renderPassDescrip
```

```
tor)!
        renderEncoder.label = "render encoder"

        renderEncoder.pushDebugGroup("draw morphing triangle")
        renderEncoder.setRenderPipelineState(pipelineState)
        renderEncoder.setVertexBuffer(vertexBuffer, offset:
        256*bufferIndex, atIndex: 0)
        renderEncoder.setVertexBuffer(vertexColorBuffer, offset:0
        , atIndex: 1)
        renderEncoder.drawPrimitives(.Triangle, vertexStart: 0,
        vertexCount: 9, instanceCount: 1)

        renderEncoder.popDebugGroup()
        renderEncoder.endEncoding()
```

First, we created the `commandBuffer` object using the instance method `commandBuffer` in the command queue that we created earlier. Then, we created the render encoder and specified the `pipelineState`, `vertextBuffer`, and `vertextColorBuffer` attributes that we created earlier. In the `drawPrimitives` method, we ask the GPU to draw a set of triangles based on the vertex buffer. Each triangle has nine vertices that start at index 0, and we have one triangle. After finishing configuration, we will call `endEncoding()`.

Now we are done. To make all these previous operations, we have to commit the command buffer to start execution. To do this, we call `commit()` at the end of the render method:

```
commandBuffer.presentDrawable(drawable)
commandBuffer.commit()
```

Summary

In this chapter, we talked about the new graphics framework Metal and its features. We gave a simple introduction to 3D rendering and how it works in programming and how computers deal with it. We used the project template that came with Xcode in Metal to draw a moving triangle in 3D space and tried to explain all major areas in code, such as devices, shaders, pipeline, command queue, command buffer, and game loops. In the next chapter, we will cover a very interesting topic, which is WatchKit development. You will learn how to start your Apple watch app development in Xcode and what you can deliver to the users in watch app.

6

Introduction to WatchKit

In this chapter, we will talk about a new technology, WatchKit, and a new era of wearable technologies. Now technology is a part of all aspects of our lives, even wearable objects. You can see smart watches such as the new Apple watch or glasses such as Google glass. We will go through the new WatchKit framework to learn how to extend your iPhone app functionalities to your wrist.

Apple watch

Apple watch is a new device on your wrist that can be used to extend your iPhone app functionality; you can access the most important information and respond in easy ways using the watch. The watch is now available in most countries in different styles and models so that everyone can find a watch that suits them.

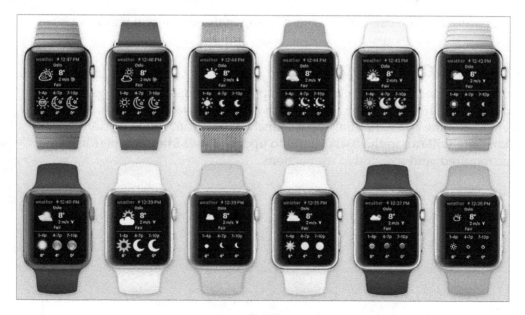

When you get your Apple watch, you can pair it with your iPhone. The watch can't be paired with the iPad; it can only be paired with your iPhone. To run third-party apps on your watch, iPhone should be paired with the watch. Once paired, when you install any app on your iPhone that has an extension for the watch, the app will be installed on the watch automatically and wirelessly.

WatchKit

WatchKit is a new framework to build apps for Apple watch. To run third-party apps on Apple watch, you need the watch to be connected to the iPhone. WatchKit helps you create apps for Apple watch by creating two targets in Xcode:

- **The WatchKit app**: The WatchKit app is an executable app to be installed on your watch, and you can install or uninstall it from your iPhone. The WatchKit app contains the storyboard file and resources files. It doesn't contain any source code, just the interface and resource files.

- **The WatchKit extension**: This extension runs on the iPhone and has the `InterfaceControllers` file for your storyboard. This extension just contains the model and controller classes. The actions and outlets from the previous WatchKit app will be linked to these controller files in the WatchKit extension.

These bundles—the WatchKit extension and WatchKit app—are put together and packed inside the iPhone application. When the user installs the iPhone app, the system will prompt the user to install the WatchKit app if there is a paired watch.

Using WatchKit, you can extend your iOS app in three different ways:

The WatchKit app

As we mentioned earlier, the WatchKit app is an app installed on Apple watch and the user can find it in the list of Watch apps. The user can launch, control, and interact with the app. Once the app is launched, the WatchKit extension on the iPhone app will run in the background to update a user interface, perform any logic required, and respond to user actions.

Note that the iPhone app can't launch or wake up the WatchKit extension or the WatchKit app. However, the WatchKit extension can ask the system to launch the iPhone app and this will be performed in the background.

Glances

Glances are single interfaces that the user can navigate between. The glance view is just read-only information, which means that you can't add any interactive UI controls such as buttons and switches. Apps should use glances to display very important and timely information. The glance view is a nonscrolling view, so your glance view should fit the watch screen. Avoid using tables and maps in interface controllers and focus on delivering the most important information in a nice way. Once the user clicks on the glance view, the watch app will be launched. The glance view is optional in your app.

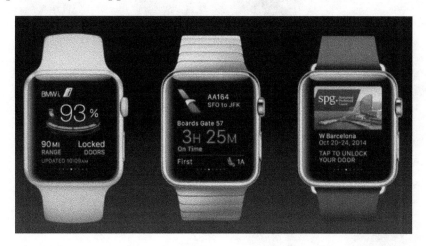

The glance interface and its interface controller files are a part of your WatchKit extension and WatchKit app. The glance interface resides in a storyboard, which resides in the WatchKit app. The interface controller that is responsible for filling the view with the timely important information is located in the WatchKit extension, which runs in the background in the iPhone app, as we said before.

Actionable notifications

For sure, you can handle and respond to local and remote notifications in an easy and fast way using Apple watch. WatchKit helps you build user interfaces for the notification that you want to handle in your WatchKit app. WatchKit helps you add actionable buttons so that the user can take action based on the notification. For example, if a notification for an invitation is sent to you, you can take action to accept or reject the notification from your wrist. You can respond to these actions easily in interface controllers in WatchKit extension.

Working with WatchKit

Enough talking about theory, lets see some action.

1. Go to our lovely Xcode and create a new single-view application and name it `WatchKitDemo`. Don't forget to select Swift as the app language. Then navigate to **File** | **New** | **Target** to create a new target for the WatchKit app:

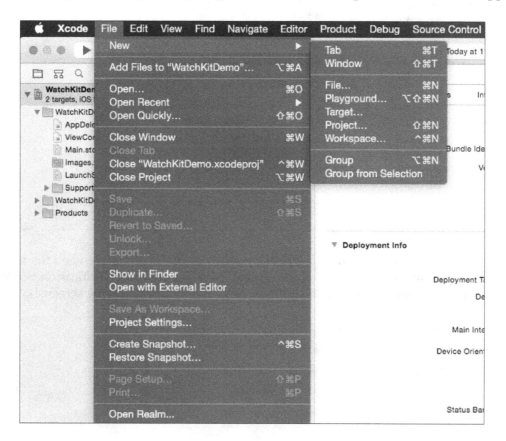

2. After you select the target, in the pop-up window, from the left side under **iOS** choose **Apple Watch** and select **WatchKit App**. Check the following screenshot:

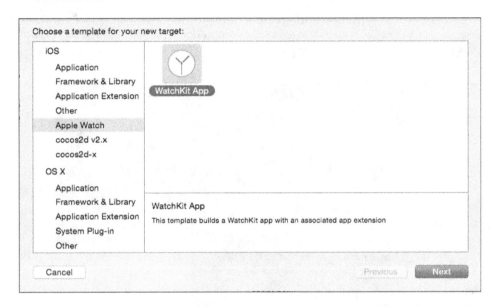

3. After you click on **Next**, it will ask you which application to embed the target in and which scenes to include. Please check the **Include Notification Scene** and **Include Glance Scene** options, as shown in the following screenshot:

4. Click on **Finish**, and now you have an iPhone app with the built-in WatchKit extension and WatchKit app.

Xcode targets

Now your project should be divided into three parts. Check the following screenshot and let's explain these parts:

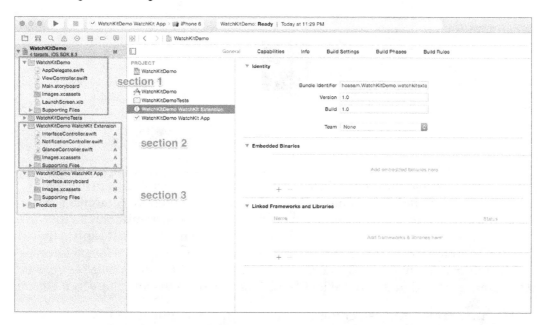

As you see in this screenshot, the project files are divided into three sections. In section 1, you can see the iPhone app source files, interface files or storyboard, and resources files. In section 2, you can find the WatchKit extension, which contains only interface controllers and model files. Again, as we said before, this extension also runs in iPhone in the background. In section 3, you can see the WatchKit app, which runs in Apple watch itself. As we see, it contains the storyboard and resources files. No source code can be added in this target.

Interface controllers

In the WatchKit extension of your Xcode project, open `InterfaceController.swift`. You will find the interface controller file for the scene that exists in `Interface.storyboard` in the WatchKit app.

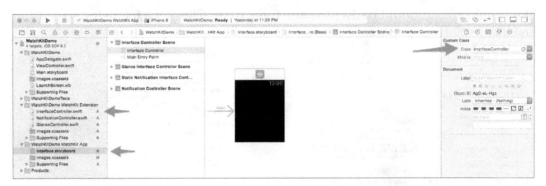

The `InterfaceController` file extends from `WKInterfaceController`, which is the base class for interface controllers. Forget the UI classes that you were using in the iOS apps from the UIKit framework, as it has different interface controller classes in WatchKit and they are very limited in configuration and customization. In the `InterfaceController` file, you can find three important methods that explain the lifecycle of your controller: `awakeWithContext`, `willActivate`, and `didDeactivate`. Another important method that can be overridden for the lifecycle is called `init`, but it's not implemented in the controller file. Let's now explain the four lifecycle methods:

- `init`: You can consider this as your first chance to update your interface elements.

- `awakeWithContext`: This is called after the `init` method and contains context data that can be used to update your interface elements or to perform some logical operations on these data. Context data is passed between interface controllers when you push or present another controller and you want to pass some data.

- `willActivate`: Here, your scene is about to be visible onscreen, and its your last chance to update your UI. Try to put simple UI changes here in this method so as not to cause freezing in UI.

- `didDeactivate`: Your scene is about to be invisible and, if you want to clean up your code, it's time to stop animations or timers.

Interface elements

We talked about the interface controller and its lifecycle. Let's now talk about interface elements in WatchKit and how they are different from UI components in UIKit. You can create scenes in a storyboard file and assign them a corresponding interface controller from the WatchKit extension. You can add multiple scenes in storyboard and change its size classes because Apple watch comes in two different sizes: 38 mm and 40 mm.

In WatchKit, the layout is completely different from the layout in iOS apps. In iOS, you can add views and change their positions in space, and then you have full control. In WatchKit, you add the components and let Xcode arrange them vertically in the scene like a stack. Then you can adjust the position and size of the component, but that too in a very limited way. For example, in a horizontal position you can choose from left, center, and right. In size, you can set fixed size, fit content, or relative to container.

Let's see this in action. Open the first scene in `Interface.storyboard` and let's add a label:

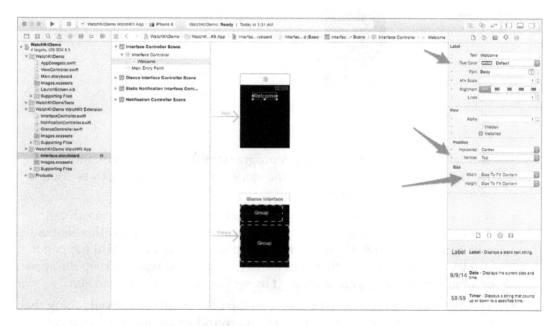

As you see in screenshot, I added a label that is the instance of the WKInterfaceLabel class and adjusted its position to be top-center in the Attribute Inspector. The Attribute Inspector here, as you can see, is totally different from the one you can see in UILabel in UIKit. The + symbol that you see lets you add specific values for different size classes. For example, you may set the font size to be 10 in 38-mm watches and 12 in 40-mm watches. Try playing with the components, and you will see how Xcode arranges them vertically for you like a stack. Here are some points I want you to take into consideration while working with interface elements:

- You can't customize interface elements by extending the base class as we were doing in iOS apps. You can add your custom UILabel by adding a new class extending from the UILabel class. In WatchKit, you can't do something like that if you try to open the identity inspector of the label that we added, you will see that the **Class** field can't be edited:

- You can't create interface elements programmatically. All scenes and interfaces can be created only via the storyboard and no code can be used to create any interface element.

- If you have a stack of elements and want to hide an element, you can call setHidden(true). In that case, other interface elements below this element will be moved automatically up to fill its place. The opposite will happen if you try to show it again; they will move down. If you want to keep the space of a hidden element, you can hide it by setting the alpha value to zero.

- You can't overlap interface elements on top of each other. The only thing that can be done is to use **Group** to set a background image for some elements.

- There is no any layer customization like we have in UIKit by adjusting CALayer. There is nothing similar in WatchKit, as these elements don't extend the UIView form.

Groups

In WatchKit, we have an awesome and very important element called **Group**. The Group element is just a container of other elements, but it has a feature that lets you arrange these elements vertically or horizontally. You can make the size of elements inside Group relative to group itself. Groups can be nested, and by default, Group has no visual representation. You can specify a background image or background color to it. This feature can be used to specify a background image to some elements by placing them inside Group. Let's now see an example of how to use Group:

1. Open the interface controller and, below the label we added before, drag **Group** from the Object library in the right-hand side and drop it.

2. Check its Attribute Inspector; you will find settings for its layout, background color/image, position, and size. Here, we will choose the **Horizontal** layout to add two images beside each other inside **Group**:

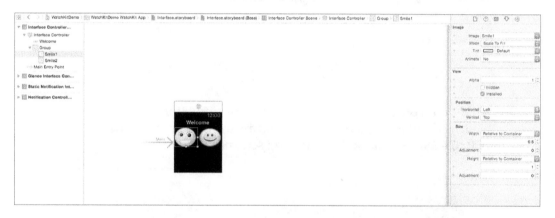

I have added two images inside **Group** and as you can see, they are added horizontally as we set in the layout. If you chose vertically, they will be added above each other.

In Attribute Inspector the size of each image is set to be relative to the container (Group), so each one will be 50 percent width and 100 percent height.

3. Now, to run on a simulator, please choose the **WatchKitDemo WatchKit App** target and click on **Run**. Check the following screenshot:

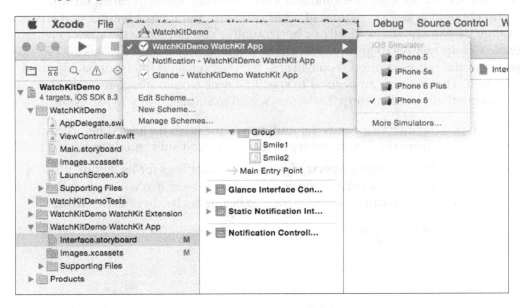

4. After you have selected Run, to display the simulator for Apple watch, open the iOS simulator and navigate to **Hardware | External Displays | Apple Watch – 38mm**. Check the following screenshot:

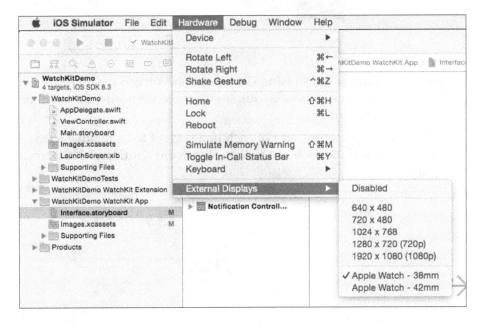

5. Now to build and run again, you should see a small simulator for Apple watch. It will look like something like this:

Navigating interfaces

Your app can contain multiple numbers of interface controllers; for sure, you need to navigate between them. In WatchKit, we have two styles used for navigation between interface controllers, and they are mutually exclusive:

- **Pages-based**: In this style, you have two or more interface controllers and only one is displayed on the screen at a time. The user can easily navigate between them by swiping left and right. A dot indicator will be displayed automatically at the bottom to indicate which page is displayed now. The page-based style can be created only in the storyboard by linking the interface controllers together with the next-page segue.

- **Hierarchical**: This style is the same as UINavigationController in UIKit. You have a root interface controller, and you can push and pop between controllers. A small back button will be displayed automatically in the top-left corner to navigate back. You can push to another interface controller via the push segue in the storyboard or programmatically by calling pushControllerWithName(name, context:). The name, as we said before, is the interface controller name in its Attribute Inspector in the storyboard.

Presenting modally

As we said, we have two styles for navigation that are mutually exclusive. Alternatively, you can interrupt the flow of navigation to present an interface controller to ask for confirmation or display information. In that case, you can present any interface controller modally from any other interface controller, regardless of the navigation style that you are using.

You can present more than one interface controller at a time. These interface controllers will be in page-based style and can't be in hierarchical style. In the next topic, you will see the different ways of presenting them modally.

To present interface controllers modally, you have three ways:

- `Modal`: In storyboard, use the `modal` segue to connect it to the interface controller that you want to present. In the event you want to present multiple interface controllers in storyboard, link these controllers with the `next-page` segue first as we mentioned earlier. Then link the `modal` segue to the first interface controller in the page flow.

- Calling `presentControllerWithName(name:, context:)`: Call this method programmatically to present a single interface controller modally given its interface name.

- Calling `presentControllerWithNames(names: , contexts:)`: Call this method programmatically to present more than one interface controller modally in a `page-based` style.

The presented modal interface has text in the top-left corner with the interface's controller name. This name can be set from the Attribute Inspector of the interface controller. When the user clicks on this title, the modal interface controller will be dismissed. You can set this title to `Done`, `Ok`, `Close`, or anything you need. If you didn't specify any name, it will be `Cancel` by default. You can programmatically dismiss the modal interface controller by calling `dismissController()`.

Let's see these navigation styles in action. In the first interface controller, add two buttons. The first one is to push a new interface controller, and the second one to present three interface controllers in a `page-based` style. Drag a new interface controller from the Object library now. Add a push segue from the first button to this new interface controller. In this new interface controller, add a label and button called **Increment**. We will add some logic to make this label read the initial value; when clicked, the button will increment this value and update the UI. Your storyboard should be like this now:

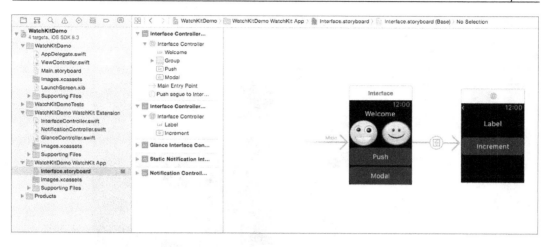

Now, in the WatchKit extension, create a new interface controller called
`SecondInterfaceController` and set the class of the new interface controller in
storyboard to `SecondInterfaceController`. In this case, we can take an outlet to
the label and set an action for the button to increment and update the UI:

Make sure that the new class is a subclass of `WKInterfaceController` and not `UIViewController`. Now link the outlet for the label and action for button:

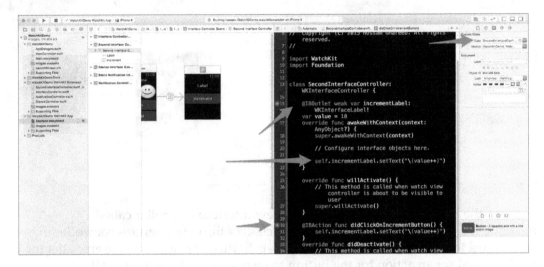

As you see, we updated the label in the `awakeWithContext` method by calling `setText()`.

Return to the storyboard to add the `modal` segue. First, drag three interface controllers and link them together with the `next-page` segues. Add a label in each interface controller and set its text with `Page 1`, `Page 2,` and `Page 3`. Then, link the second button to the first interface controller in the pages flow. Your storyboard should be like this now:

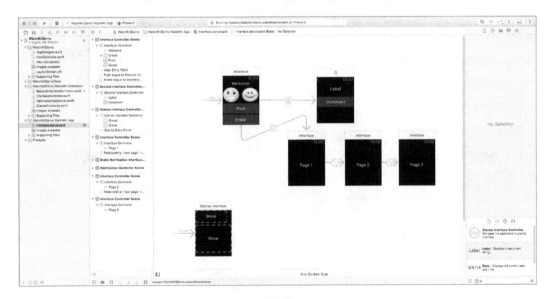

Now to build and run, you should see something like this in the push and modal styles:

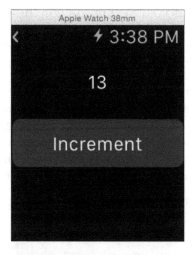

Animation

Creating animation in WatchKit is not like using core animation or anything equivalent. To present an animation on screen in WatchKit, you have to use GIF technology to animate a series of images. For example, to display an animated circular progress bar on screen, you have to generate an image for each state. In the circular progress bar, you can generate 100 images and animate the, from image #0 to image #60 if you want to display 60 percent progress and so on. Check the next section of glances, where we will display the animated progress bar in the glance interface controller.

Working with glances

We talked about glances earlier as they are a simple interface to display timely and important information such as your next meeting in the Calendar app and your remaining tasks in the To Do app. The glance interface is read-only and can't include any interactive controls. Just tapping on glance view will launch your WatchKit app. Glances are optional in your WatchKit app.

Now let's see how to build an interface for the glance screen and how to test it in a simulator. Open storyboard and you should see a prepared `InterfaceController` for glance with a glance start point. Its interface controller is called `GlanceController`. `swift` and is located in the WatchKit extension. Xcode comes with built-in templates for the glance screen. To see these templates, select the **Glance Interface Controller** and click on **Attribute Inspector**. You will see templates for **Upper** and **Lower** Groups:

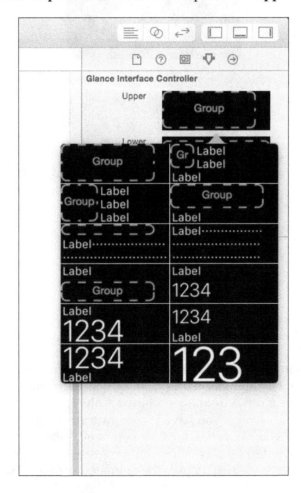

The templates will be displayed to you after you click on the Group that you want to customize. Now leave the default templates and, in the upper Group, add an image and date label. In WatchKit, it has a built-in `WKInterfaceDate` to display the current date and time and it updates itself automatically. The scene up to now will be something like this:

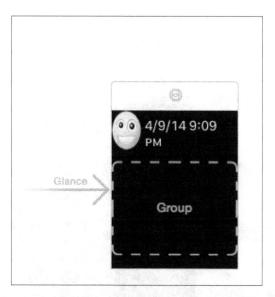

Then, in the lower Group, we will display the animated circular progress bar. As we said, we need a series of images to be displayed as WatchKit doesn't support animation. You can visit this website at `http://hmaidasani.github.io/RadialChartImageGenerator/`. It lets you fully customize the circular bar and generates the image for you. In the website, it gives you the option to add middle text and its value will be animated. If you need a special effect for text to control its customization, you can remove the text from the images and add the text as a label in interface builder above the progress image. But to do so, the image has to be a group background image, as you can't interface controllers that can't be flipped above each other. Drag an outlet for the lower Group to set the background image to it:

```
override func willActivate() {
    // This method is called when watch view controller is
    about to be visible to user
    self.progressGroup.setBackgroundImageNamed("progress")
    self.progressGroup.startAnimatingWithImagesInRange
    (NSMakeRange(0, 75), duration: 0.7, repeatCount: 1)

    super.willActivate()
}
```

Now the images will be animated starting from image #0 to image #75 over 0.7 seconds with repeating count 1. To build and run the glance, you have to choose it first from the list of targets as we did while running the Watch app:

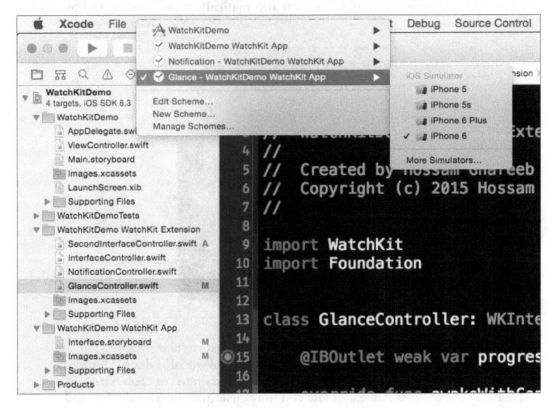

After you run it, you should see something like this:

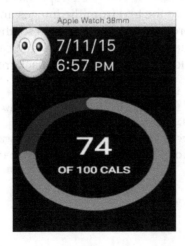

Summary

In this chapter, we covered a very important topic: how to develop apps for the new wearable technology, Apple watch. We first gave a quick introduction about the new device and how it can communicate with paired iPhones. We then talked about WatchKit, the new framework, that enables you to develop apps for Apple watch and design its interface. We saw how it's far more limited than UIKit because you are constrained with a small screen size and very limited resources. Apple has designed the watch to contain only the storyboard and resources files. All logic and operations are performed in the iPhone app in the background. Finally, we saw different ways to create interface controllers, how to build your layout, and different styles of navigation between the interface controllers. In the next chapter we will talk about iOS 8 app extensions. Stay tuned!

7
Swift App Extensions

We are still working with the new features and APIs introduced in iOS 8. In this chapter, we are going to talk about app extensions. App extensions are meant to give you the ability to extend your app functionality to be accessible outside your app while users use other apps or the system. In iOS 8, many extensions have been released, and in this chapter, we will talk about all these extensions. You can then decide on which extension to use, and when.

App extensions

As we said, an app extension is just a task that can be performed and accessed outside you app. For example, you can use an extension to display timely content in the Today view of the notification center.

An extension for the sports app displays the currently playing games and results. This data can be updated in real time and can really help users to reach their content in an easy and fast way and from any place—the system or other apps.

Another extension gives you the ability to add a custom keyboard that replaces the boring system keyboard. Users can choose which keyboard to activate choose the one that appeals to them, and make their writing experience easier. App extensions are introduced in iOS 8 and OS X 10.10, so some extensions exist in both iOS and OS X, some of them in iOS only, and some are in OS X only. Here, we will list all available app extensions that are available in iOS. All the upcoming extensions are easy to use, thanks to Xcode, as it provides you with a working template once you create the extension target from Xcode.

Today

The **Today** extension (always called a widget) is an extension for both iOS and OS X. As we have seen in the previous example, this extension is used for displaying content or to perform tasks from the Today view of the notification center.

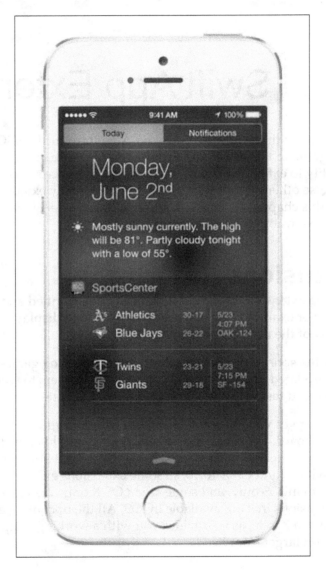

The widget should be used to display important information, timely updated content, or provide easy access to your app tasks. This extension will be very useful in many kinds of apps. In the weather app, you can see an extension that displays weather information for your current location. In the Sports app like the previous screenshot, you can display the current game results and top news or transfers between clubs. In the To Do app, you can see your to-do list for today, and you can easily mark tasks as done through the widget or create a new task very rapidly.

Users can access their widget by swiping down their screen, and the **Notification/ Today** screen will be displayed. You can see the widgets in the **Today** view. The **Today** view can also be accessed even if your iPhone is locked, but you have to enable it from **Settings**. Navigate to **Settings | Touch ID & Passcode**; then you can enable or disable the **Today** view.

Before starting to work with the **Today** widget, here are some notes to take into consideration:

- **Content should be up-to-date**: The content that you are going to add should be up to date because this widget is accessible from anywhere and the user expects to see something new or important when he opens the **Today** view.

- **Simple and important content**: The content should also be important as we said, and at the same time, it should be simple. Don't crowd the widget with controls or unnecessary content.

- **Don't add scroll view in the widget**: The **Today** view itself is scrollable to contain all the available widgets, so adding one scroll view inside another scroll view will really confuse the user. Believe me, he/she will remove your widget from the **Today** view.

- **Memory usage**: Take into account that the system will easily kill/terminate your widget if it causes memory pressure or doesn't use memory wisely.

- **No keyboard support**: You can take the keyboard input through the **Today** widget.

The user is able to edit the **Today** view to choose which widgets to be displayed and can reorder them. It will be nice to let users edit and customize their widget through your app. For example, in a sports app, the user can choose which league results to be displayed or even which sport he is interested in if the app supports multiple sports. Another example is the weather app, in which the user can choose the cities whose weather he/she is interested in.

Share

The **Share** extension is a very simple extension that is available in both iOS and OS X. This extension lets your users share their content through your app so that you can then post this data in a social network or send it via any API service. In any app, when the user clicks on the **Share** button, a native activity view controller will be displayed to select which share extension to share it in. For sure, there are native ones such as Mail, SMS, Facebook, and Twitter. You can add your own extension as well.

When you work with the Share extension and a user chooses your extension to share the content, the extension lets you use the system-provided compose view by default, which is very similar to the one used in sharing with Facebook or Twitter. If the system doesn't meet your needs or you have some options or settings that can be selected in the composer, you have the option to provide your own UI. In the following screenshot, you will see a sample of the native compose view that your app extension can use by default:

Photo Editing

This extension is available in iOS only and enables users to edit their photos or videos from the Photos native app using the Photo Editing extension. After selecting the Photo Editing extension and applying changes to the photo, the new content (a new version of the photo or video) will be available in the Photos app. For security, the Photos app will always keep the original version of your photo or video.

The following screenshot is an example of a Photo Editing extension that can be opened directly from the Photos app:

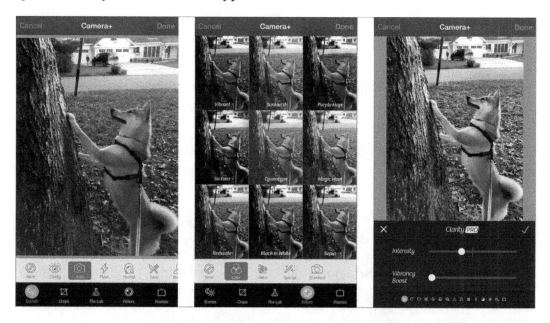

The Photo Editing extension is meant for editing photos and videos and not other operations such as sharing. Use other extensions if your task is not mainly for editing media contents. Before working with the Photo Editing extension, here is a list of some points to take care about:

- The Photos app keeps the original version, the current version (new photo after editing), and the set of adjustments that have been applied to the original version.

- When the user selects the Photo Editing extension to edit an asset, the Photos app asks the extension if it can read the set of adjustments. If the extension can support these adjustments, the Photos app will provide the original photo as an input and the extension can let the users set, revert, or add new edits. If the extension doesn't support these adjustments, the Photos app will provide the final version of the photo and in that case the user can only apply new edits.

- For videos, the Photos app saves only the original content and, if the extension can't read the adjustments data, it has to deal with the original content.

- Once the extension is selected, a custom view for the Photo Editing extension will be displayed with its custom interface. The view controller that will be used as an extension should conform to the `PHContentEditingController` protocol.

- In your app, add only one extension for each media type as the Photos app will display only a maximum of 1 extension for each media type for a single app.

- Don't add a navigation bar in your interface of extension, as it will be shown automatically by the Photos app.

- Write high-quality and high-performance code to edit media types as the extension is going to deal with high-resolution contents.

Document Provider

This extension is available in iOS only. The Document Provider extension is used by apps that are dealing with specific document type. In the Document Provider extension, you store documents for a particular type and other apps can access these files. The Document Provider has a shared container to save these files, and other apps can export documents easily to this shared container. Any app can access the Document Provider files using a document picker view controller.

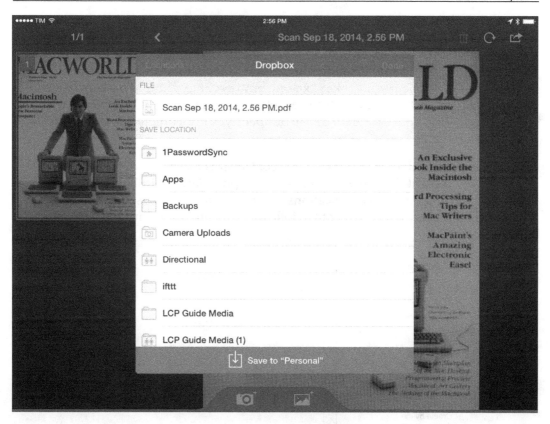

The Document Provider extension consists of two parts:

- **Document picker view controller**: This provides your Document Provider's user interface. The system displays this picker controller interface when any app presents a document picker view controller for your document provider. The picker interface allows users to browse and select documents from inside your document provider. This extension can also perform basic import and export operations.

- **File provider**: The file provider extension has no interface in it, and you must create this extension if you are going to support open and move operations. This extension grants the host app access to files outside its sandbox.

Like all the other extensions, Xcode helps you a lot in getting started with extensions by providing templates. So once you go to targets and add a new one, then choose the **Document Provider** extension. Two extensions will be generated for you: **Document Picker** and **File Provider**. In document picker view controller, it must be a subclass of `UIDocumentPickerExtensionViewController`. This subclass will automatically be instantiated once a user selects your Document Provider extension from `UIDocumentMenuViewController` or opens your document provider directly from `UIDocumentPickerViewController`.

Anyway, once your document picker view controller is instantiated, the system will automatically present this view controller in the app's view controller. It also provides you with a navigation bar with **Locations** and **Done** buttons. Thus, you don't have to add a navigation bar. Take a look at the following screenshot for more clarification:

Understanding the Document Provider's lifecycle

It's very important to understand the lifecycle and states of your Document Provider extensions, as your extension will be used with other apps. Take a look at the following screenshot for the lifecycle of the Document Provider extension:

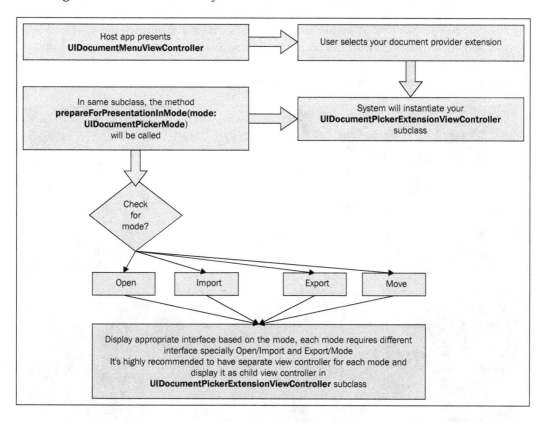

From the preceding screenshot, we can see the lifecycle of the Document Provider extension and how you have to interact with the four modes: open, import, export, and move. As we said, each mode has a different interface as each mode has different functionality.

The custom keyboard

The custom keyboard extension is an extension for iOS only, as its functionality is replacing the boring system keyboard with a custom keyboard. You may create this extension to support languages that are still not supported in the iOS or to provide a smarter, easier, fancier, or customizable keyboard for users. When you decide to use this extension, you have to be aware that this keyboard is a system-wide keyboard. If the user selects it as the default keyboard, it will be available in all third-party apps and system apps. Note that this keyboard is not specifically for your app or to make life easier while using your app only. It will be system-wide, as we said.

Before you decide to go with the custom keyboard, you should note the following:

- Your keyboard will be system-wide.
- You must provide an option for users to switch to another keyboard. It displays the globe key that switches your keyboard to another one when you click on it, like the system keyboard.

- Study the system keyboard well and learn how it changes itself to help users. For example, if the layout is changed based on UIKeyboardType, when you write an e-mail, you will find a new key appears for @, and pressing. for a while will display a list of common used domains. So be aware of keyboard types.

- Your keyboard should be fast and responsive. Avoid any interruption to the user while using your keyboard.

- Handle autocapitalization at the beginning of sentences.

- Any settings, customization, or any other interactions should be placed in your app.

- Features such as handling suggestions, autocomplete, autocorrection, and so on should be considered.

- You are responsible for handling all the previous features; there are no system APIs for these.

Keyboard security

For security and privacy, in some cases, your custom keyboard will not be available and will be replaced with the system keyboard. In all fields that have secure text such as password fields, when the user starts to type, the system keyboard will be displayed temporarily and your custom keyboard will be back after the user selects another field. Also, in fields that have keyboard types such as UIKeyboardTypePhonePad or UIKeyboardTypeNamePhonePad, keyboards will be replaced with the system one.

Anyone can reject the use of all the custom keyboards in this app—for example, banking apps or apps that deal with sensitive data. To do so, you have to override the shouldAllowExtensionPointIdentifier: method in AppDelegate like this:

```
func application(application: UIApplication,
shouldAllowExtensionPointIdentifier extensionPointIdentifier:
String) -> Bool {
    return false
}
```

Another thing to know is that your keyboard extension has no access to the microphone.

Trust is very important in your custom keyboard. When a user uses your custom keyboard, you have access to what users are typing while using your keyboard.

Keyboard settings

Any keyboard should have some settings such as autocorrections, enable swiping, or shortcuts. When you navigate to **Settings | General | Keyboard** in an iOS device, you will see the settings of the system keyboard. Your custom keyboard has no settings like this and can't be accessed from here. You can add settings to your custom keyboard in the containing app or in the **Create Settings** bundle for your extension, and it can then be accessed from **Settings**.

Working with the custom keyboard

Before starting to work with the custom keyboard extension, you need to know the architecture of your extension and how things work. Take a look at the following screenshot:

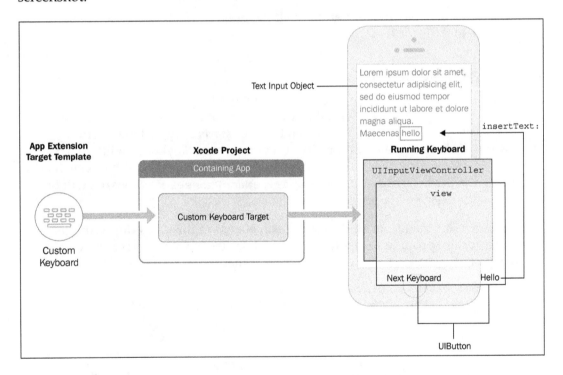

As you can see, your containing app contains the extension (the custom keyboard target) and, when a user starts to edit a field, the custom keyboard appears. You will have a subclass of UIInputViewController, which is the primary view controller in your extension. Then you can add gestures or any interface controls to its property inputView.

Creating a new target for the custom keyboard in Xcode manages most things for you. You will find a subclass of UIInputViewController and configurations in the info.plist file. You will find a prepared button for switching keyboards, as this is the most important one, as well. By default, the keyboard has no access to an Internet connection or to share a container with the containing app as these may affect the trust between the keyboard extension and the user. To enable these, set the value of the RequestsOpenAccess key to YES in the info.plist file.

There is a very important property in UIInputViewController: textDocumentProxy. The textDocumentProxy property is the proxy to the text input object (for example, a text field) that your custom keyboard interacts with. Here are some examples of how to use it to insert text or delete the text backward:

```
var proxy = self.textDocumentProxy as! UITextDocumentProxy
proxy.insertText("Hi there, ")   // Inserting text
proxy.insertText("\n")           // Inserting new line
proxy.deleteBackward()           //  Delete a character from
the displayed text
```

As we said earlier, you have to respond to the change of UIKeyboardType so the layout should be changed based on the keyboard type. As well, your keyboard can support multilanguages and you can do this by providing a separate keyboard for each language; in that case, you will have multiple targets or can handle the process dynamically and switch the layout when the primary language is changed.

Demo

Working with the app extensions is not a big deal, and Xcode templates help you so much to get started with your extension. In this section, we will build a very simple demo on one of the preceding extensions: the Today extension. We talked about the Today widget and saw how it's very helpful to provide your users with appropriately updated data in an easier way from the Today view in the notification center.

So, in this demo we are going to make a widget that displays weather information. We will display the weather for Venice. As you know, it's just a demo, but in the real world you can use location services to display the weather data of the user's current city. Also, maybe you can display a list of weather data for multiple cities that the user sets as his favorites in your containing app.

1. Okay, now it's playtime. Create a new Xcode project with any template and choose Swift as the language. Then navigate to **File | New | Target**. Take a look at the following screenshot:

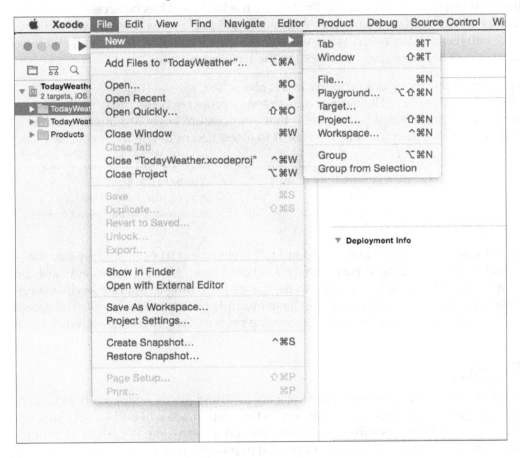

2. Then, under **iOS**, select **Application Extension** and choose **Today Extension**:

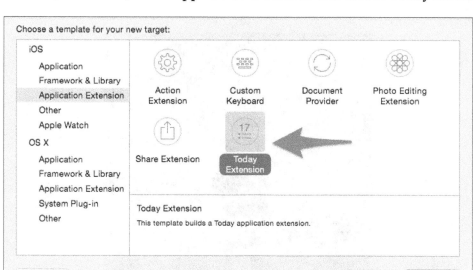

3. Choose **Swift** as the language and set the name as `TodayWidget`. Now a new target will be created for you. In the `TodayWidget` folder, you will see two important files: `TodayViewController.swift` and `MainInterface.storyboard`. These files are the controller and interface builder for your widget.

4. As mentioned earlier, the Xcode template prepares everything for you. So, to justify that, select **TodayWidget** as the active scheme target and click on **Run**:

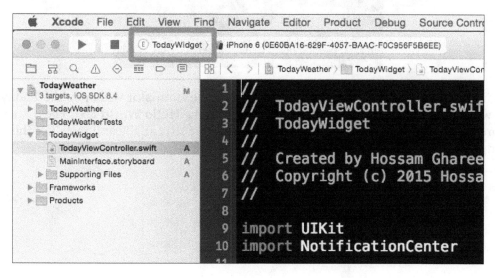

Now, in a simulator, you will see something like this:

As in the preceding screenshot, you will see that the simulator will open the **Today** view for you and your widget appears there with the **Hello World** text. The display name of the extension can be changed from the Info.plist file and the UI of the widget will be loaded from the storyboard file.

Now we are going to request the weather data for Venice, and then bind this data in the UI. I have used this API service; it's free for limited data. You can create an account just to get the API key to be used in requests. Let's now create a new Swift class called `WeatherManager.swift`, as our model manager. It will connect to the server to send requests and get the updated current weather for the given city. Before going with it, visit `http://www.worldweatheronline.com/api/docs/local-city-town-weather-api.aspx` to learn how to build the API request and what the available parameters and responses are. Take a look at the following code to learn how we have built our `WeatherManager` class:

```swift
let weatherKey = "add_your_key_here"

class WeatherInfo{
    let cityName:String
    let tempC:String
    let weatherDesc:String
    let weatherIcon:String

    init(city:String, tempc:String, weatherDesc:String,
    iconURL:String){
        self.cityName = city
        self.tempC = tempc
        self.weatherDesc = weatherDesc
        self.weatherIcon = iconURL
    }
}


typealias weatherResponseHandler = (info:WeatherInfo!,
error:NSError!) -> (Void)

class WeatherManager: NSObject {

  func getWeatherForCity(city:String,
  handler:weatherResponseHandler){

      let url = NSURL(string:
      "https://api.worldweatheronline.com/free/v2/
      weather.ashx?key=\(weatherKey)&q=\(city)&format=json")

      NSURLConnection.sendAsynchronousRequest(NSURLRequest(URL:
      url!), queue: NSOperationQueue.mainQueue()) { (response,
      data, error) -> Void in
```

```
if error == nil{
    let jsonStr = NSString(data: data, encoding:
    NSUTF8StringEncoding) // response as string


    var jsonObj =
    NSJSONSerialization.JSONObjectWithData(data,
    options: NSJSONReadingOptions.AllowFragments,
    error: nil) as! NSDictionary
    jsonObj = jsonObj["data"] as! NSDictionary
    var requestData = jsonObj["request"] as! NSArray
    var queryData = requestData[0] as! NSDictionary
    let currentConditionData =
    jsonObj["current_condition"] as! NSArray
    let currentCondition = currentConditionData[0] as!
    NSDictionary

    let cityName = queryData["query"] as! String
    let tempC = currentCondition["temp_C"] as! String
    let weatherDescData : NSDictionary =
    (currentCondition["weatherDesc"] as!
    NSArray).objectAtIndex(0) as! NSDictionary
    let weatherDesc = weatherDescData["value"] as!
    String
    let weatherIconData : NSDictionary =
    (currentCondition["weatherIconUrl"] as!
    NSArray).objectAtIndex(0) as! NSDictionary
    let weatherIconURL = weatherIconData["value"] as!
    String

    let info = WeatherInfo(city: cityName, tempc:
    tempC, weatherDesc: weatherDesc, iconURL:
    weatherIconURL)

    handler(info: info, error: nil)
}
else{
    handler(info: nil, error: error)
}


        }
    }
}
```

As we have seen, we built a class called `WeatherInfo` to bind the needed information to be displayed in the weather widget. Then we created the `WeatherManager` class that has a function called `getWeatherForCity` that takes the city name and a closure. We explained closure in earlier chapters and used it here to pass the block of code with parameters, which will be `WeatherInfo` after parsing the response and an error if something wrong happened. Then we build the API request and send the request asynchronously so as not to block the main thread. In API, you can set the format of response that you prefer: XML or JSON. We parsed the JSON response and bound the needed information in the `WeatherInfo` object.

Now it's time to build a simple UI to display this information in the Today widget. Open storyboard and add an image and labels to display weather data. It should be something like this:

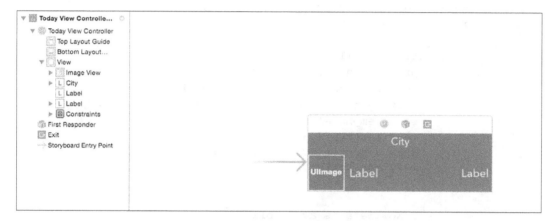

Then link the outlets in `TodayWidgetViewController` to update the UI. We defined the outlets and the `WeatherManager` object like this:

```
@IBOutlet weak var cityNameLabel: UILabel!

    @IBOutlet weak var weatherImageView: UIImageView!

    @IBOutlet weak var weatherDescLabel: UILabel!

    @IBOutlet weak var tempLabel: UILabel!
    let manager = WeatherManager()
```

Then, you should find the function called
`widgetPerformUpdateWithCompletionHandler,` in which you should add your
updates such as requesting the weather and updating the UI:

```
func widgetPerformUpdateWithCompletionHandler(completionHandler:
((NCUpdateResult) -> Void)!) {
        // Perform any setup necessary in order to update the
        view.

        // If an error is encountered, use NCUpdateResult.Failed
        // If there's no update required, use
        NCUpdateResult.NoData
        // If there's an update, use NCUpdateResult.NewData

        manager.getWeatherForCity("Venice", handler: { (info,
        error) -> (Void) in

            if error == nil{
                println(info.cityName)
                self.cityNameLabel.text = info.cityName
                self.weatherDescLabel.text = info.weatherDesc
                self.tempLabel.text = "\(info.tempC)°"
                self.weatherImageView.image = UIImage(data:
                NSData(contentsOfURL: NSURL(string:
                info.weatherIcon)!)!)


                //Now data is available
            }

        })
        completionHandler(NCUpdateResult.NewData)
}
```

As we saw, we requested the weather for Venice, and, in the completion closure,
we updated the UI. Override the following functions to change the height of your
widget based on your content. As we said before, don't use `UIScrollView`. The code
should be like this:

```
override func viewWillAppear(animated: Bool) {

        var size = self.preferredContentSize
        size.height = 100
        self.preferredContentSize = size
}
```

```
func
widgetMarginInsetsForProposedMarginInsets(defaultMarginInsets:
UIEdgeInsets) -> UIEdgeInsets {
    return UIEdgeInsetsZero
}
```

The edge inset is set to zero to make the widget fill the content size. Now build and run the code, and you should see something like this:

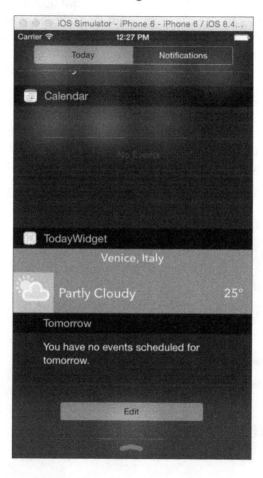

Summary

In this chapter, we talked about iOS app extensions and which one you should use to meet your requirements. Extensions give a new flavor to the iOS to make the user reach your app functionality while using other apps. We talked about the Today widget and how it's useful to display timely information when the user opens the Today view in the notification center. We then saw how apps can share content via the Share extension of your app. If your app has a functionality to open and manage specific documents, you can use the Document Provider extension and let other apps use your extension to open, browse, or export contents. We also saw the awesome custom keyboard extension that lets you design the new keyboard to be system-wide and replace the system keyboard. Finally, we implemented a demo in one of these extensions: the Today extension. We displayed the current weather of the beautiful city of Venice in the Today screen.

I hope that this book has provided you with the information you need to master the Swift language and use it in all your upcoming projects. I hope this book also is a good guide for you in using the new technologies in iOS 8 with Swift, and wish you success and glory in your life and career path!

Index

Thank you for buying
Application Development with Swift

About Packt Publishing

Packt, pronounced 'packed', published its first book, *Mastering phpMyAdmin for Effective MySQL Management*, in April 2004, and subsequently continued to specialize in publishing highly focused books on specific technologies and solutions.

Our books and publications share the experiences of your fellow IT professionals in adapting and customizing today's systems, applications, and frameworks. Our solution-based books give you the knowledge and power to customize the software and technologies you're using to get the job done. Packt books are more specific and less general than the IT books you have seen in the past. Our unique business model allows us to bring you more focused information, giving you more of what you need to know, and less of what you don't.

Packt is a modern yet unique publishing company that focuses on producing quality, cutting-edge books for communities of developers, administrators, and newbies alike. For more information, please visit our website at www.packtpub.com.

About Packt Open Source

In 2010, Packt launched two new brands, Packt Open Source and Packt Enterprise, in order to continue its focus on specialization. This book is part of the Packt Open Source brand, home to books published on software built around open source licenses, and offering information to anybody from advanced developers to budding web designers. The Open Source brand also runs Packt's Open Source Royalty Scheme, by which Packt gives a royalty to each open source project about whose software a book is sold.

Writing for Packt

We welcome all inquiries from people who are interested in authoring. Book proposals should be sent to author@packtpub.com. If your book idea is still at an early stage and you would like to discuss it first before writing a formal book proposal, then please contact us; one of our commissioning editors will get in touch with you.

We're not just looking for published authors; if you have strong technical skills but no writing experience, our experienced editors can help you develop a writing career, or simply get some additional reward for your expertise.

Swift Essentials

ISBN: 978-1-78439-670-1   Paperback: 228 pages

Get up and running lightning fast with this practical guide to building applications with Swift

1. Rapidly learn how to program Apple's newest programming language, Swift, from the basics through to working applications.

2. Create graphical iOS applications using Xcode and storyboard.

3. Build a network client for GitHub repositories, with full source code on GitHub.

Swift Cookbook

ISBN: 978-1-78439-137-9   Paperback: 392 pages

Over 50 hands-on recipes to help you create apps, solve problems, and build your portfolio of projects in Swift

1. Get familiar with the features of Xcode 6 with Swift to write code that is shorter, clearer, and runs faster on today's multi-core architectures.

2. Packed with practical recipes that will help you gain an extra edge and use Apple's new programming language like a professional.

3. Build your portfolio with Swift code using this hands-on guide.

Please check **www.PacktPub.com** for information on our titles

Lift Application Development
Cookbook

Lift Application Development Cookbook

ISBN: 978-1-84951-588-7   Paperback: 254 pages

Over 50 practical recipes to build web applications using Lift, the most secure web framework available

1. Lift made easy with step-by-steps recipes written by a developer for developers.

2. Practical examples covering topics from basic to advanced levels.

3. Learn to use Schemifier to automatically create tables and columns.

4. Understand how to integrate Lift with other technologies and social media.

Application Development
with Parse using iOS SDK

Application Development with Parse using iOS SDK

ISBN: 978-1-78355-033-3   Paperback: 112 pages

Develop the backend of your applications instantly using Parse iOS SDK

1. Build your applications using Parse iOS which serves as a complete cloud-based backend service.

2. Understand and write your code on cloud to minimize the load on the client side.

3. Learn how to create your own applications using Parse SDK, with the help of the step- by- step, practical tutorials.

Please check **www.PacktPub.com** for information on our titles

www.ingramcontent.com/pod-product-compliance
Lightning Source LLC
Chambersburg PA
CBHW060148060326
40690CB00018B/4029